Praise from global Enneagram teachers

Milton C. Stewart, MBA (USA) president, International Enneagram Association (IEA Global); coach, trainer, and consultant; founder of Kaizen Careers, Coaching, and Consulting; podcast host of *Do It for the Gram*

I am blown away. I've read almost every Enneagram book imaginable and have yet to see a book that is so specifically actionable for the development work of each person. What's inside? *Development by Design* has specific Enneagram concepts, theory, and practices that are usually locked away inside the wisdom of the early Enneagram teachers. Ginger changes all that, laying the information out clearly with full illustrations. She takes the complex and makes it elegantly simple, all in an easily digestible format.

Sharon K. Ball, LPC-MHSP (USA) coach, trainer, and consultant; founder of 9 Paths; co-author of *Reclaiming YOU: Using the Enneagram to Move from Trauma to Resilience*

What stands out about *Development by Design* is the book's intentional design. The reflective prompts, illustrations, and developmental pathways mirror how real transformation happens – not through information alone, but through full engagement, curiosity, and honest self-assessment. Ginger integrates the Enneagram with wisdom traditions like the Law of Three and somatic awareness, creating a developmental map that honors complexity without overwhelming. *Development by Design* is accessible without being simplistic, deep without being dogmatic, and structured without being rigid. It's your invitation to slow down, notice both your desires and your resistance, and compassionately engage with what emerges.

Peter O'Hanrahan (USA) teacher, coach, and consultant; senior faculty with Palmer-Daniels Narrative Enneagram School for over 30 years; founder of The Enneagram at Work

In *Development by Design*, Ginger has created a wonderful, innovative resource for those of us using the Enneagram for personal and professional growth. Adapting the Enneagram to the process of learning and development using the Law of Three – a theory central to the system that predates the psychological types – she's got it all in the right sequence: Foundations; Where am I now?; Where am I going?; Resistance; and Resolution. With a writing style that is both sophisticated and easy to access – and the book's skillful visual design – you are in for a treat.

Praise from global Enneagram teachers

Jennifer Joss, PhD (USA) consultant, trainer, and coach, author of *The Enneagram Symbol: Mapping the Journey of Personal, Social, and Spiritual Evolution*

I just love this book. It's amazing, really, with such an easy, inviting tone and feel, and yet it drops you into some very deep and provocative places... gently, one step at a time. Ginger managed to do in a relatively short combination book and workbook what might take days or months in an interactive process, giving the reins and the pace to the reader, which is lovely. So many specific things I like about it, not the least of which is the quality, depth, and incisive focus of the Enneagram detail, a product of Ginger's years of experience, insight, and continuous learning.

Margarita Guerra, MA, LLM (Spain) vice-president, International Enneagram Association (IEA Global); president, Spanish Enneagram Association (AEneagrama); founder of Enneagram in Company, co-author of *Negociador 365*

Many people reach a pivotal moment in their Enneagram journey: "I know my type - now what?" This is where this book truly stands apart. Ginger goes beyond insight and awareness to show how the Enneagram becomes a living, practical tool for real change. With clarity, depth, and wisdom, she guides readers to understand their starting point and to consciously design a personalized path of development, supported by thoughtful exercises and practices that make growth tangible and sustainable.

Adelaida Harrison, MA (Mexico) coach, trainer, podcast host of *Eneagrama Conócete*, author of *The Neuroscience Behind the Enneagram*

Ginger did it again. I love this book, finding it valuable in every sense. That said, its greatest differentiator lies in two innovative and wonderful qualities. First, it offers a grounded, practical, and immediately applicable guide to self-discovery while also providing a clear path for personal and professional development. Just as important, it makes this work accessible to everyone, including people who may not have access to coaching, training, or support groups. It is both empowering and sustainable.

Praise from global Enneagram teachers

Russ Hudson, MA (USA) teacher, scholar, keynote speaker, co-founder of The Enneagram Institute, co-author of multiple Enneagram books, including *The Wisdom of the Enneagram*

What is wonderful about this book is that Ginger takes you beyond the basics to understand the deeper purpose of Enneagram work, including teachings from the original framework that are not often mentioned in Enneagram books. *Development by Design* thus functions as a marvelous bridge between the fundamentals of the system and the profound ways it can serve us in awakening to our most authentic self and our true purpose in this world. With so many new voices coming into the Enneagram field, Ginger's experience and steady guidance into the soul of these teachings are welcome and much needed. Whether you are new to the Enneagram or have been exploring it for some time already, the insights in this book will be well worth your time.

Khaled ElSherbini, PhD (Egypt) founder of Consciousness Academy, author of *The Integral Enneagram Program*

In *Development by Design*, Ginger Lapid-Bogda offers a fresh and compelling contribution to the Enneagram field, bringing the developmental journey to life with her signature blend of clarity, creativity, and deep insight. Having known Ginger for many years, I felt her voice and wisdom come through these pages with a depth that is both personal and profoundly authentic. She brings the Law of Three alive as a living, breathing process, illuminating how we grow, resist, and ultimately reconcile what is most essential within us. Through its practical guidance and visually engaging design, this book offers accessible pathways for newcomers while providing deep nourishment for seasoned practitioners. This is a heartfelt and timely companion for all those who are committed to conscious development.

Jerome Wagner, PhD (USA) International Enneagram Association founder, author of *The Enneagram Spectrum of Personality Styles*; *Nine Lenses on the World: The Enneagram Perspective*; and the Wagner Enneagram Personality Style Scales (WEPSS)

Development by Design touches all the bases in Enneagram theory. It's a fine, comprehensive review whether you are new to or already proficient in the Enneagram. What it adds are abundant reflection exercises to ground the Enneagram in our experience. Ginger highlights three dynamic forces – affirming, denying, and reconciling – to catalyze the transformation from our constricted partial personality to our full real self. Enjoy the expansion.

Praise from global Enneagram teachers

Alice Yuen, MBA (Singapore) coach and trainer, author of *The Tribal Enneagram*

Development by Design doesn't just explain the Law of Three; it puts it to work. Ginger Lapid-Bogda makes you look into your desires deeply, your resistance clearly, and then find ways for integration to happen. It stays with the real work, without smoothing over the hard parts. This book asks for attention and honesty, and it rewards them with genuine movement and depth. If you're ready to move beyond observing your patterns and collecting insights and start engaging the forces that actually change them, this book paves the way to transformation.

Rev. Clare Loughrige, MMin (USA) lead pastor, Crossroads Church and Ministries; principal, Crossroads Soul Resources, School of Spiritual Direction; co-author of *Spiritual Rhythms of the Enneagram and Motions of the Soul*

What Ginger has created here is a life-book that is brilliant, beautiful, and holistic. She offers a *Development by Design* approach that dives deeply into the self with penetrating questions – questions that will not go away, demanding reflection and continual return daily, seasonally, and yearly as a way to stay present to one's truest desire: to be fully oneself. The format invites you to explore the very depths of your soul with clarity and ease, but always with a powerful, invigorating challenge. Once again, Ginger sets the bar high for us personally and professionally. I will be utilizing this work with spiritual direction clients and incorporating it as required reading in our School of Spiritual Direction.

Chloé Keric-Eli, MSc (Canada) past International Enneagram Association (IEA Global) board member, coach and trainer, founder of Dixit Ennéagramme

In an Enneagram landscape crowded with shortcuts, social-media soundbites, and surface-level insights, *Development by Design* stands apart. Ginger Lapid-Bogda skillfully weaves conceptual rigor and practical application into a mature, ethical, and deeply human invitation toward patient, sustained self-engagement. This book strikes a rare balance: it is clear and accessible, yet quietly demanding. It invites us to be real and avoid spiritual bypass and ego traps by engaging the head, heart, and body in lived experience. This book will resonate with those who find beauty in staying with paradox, complexity, and honesty, where change is never abstract, nor effortless, nor finished. It carries the grounded authority of a masterpiece: not one that tells you who to be, but one that cares for your ongoing process of becoming.

Praise from global Enneagram teachers

Anne Murée (USA) trainer, coach, founder of the Minnesota IEA Chapter, author of *Teach the Enneagram: Teach from Your Wholeness, Your Students Transform and So Do You*

I love this book. *Development by Design* is an engaging invitation to living from our wholeness. Its three-center approach, deep wisdom, and exquisite illustrations equip readers of all levels to use the Enneagram as a tool for awareness, change, and growth. Buy a copy now and use it individually or in your Enneagram growth group. Ginger has given us a golden gift, invaluable at this time.

Maggie Balboa, MSc (Egypt) past president of IEA Egypt, integral coach, family constellation facilitator, business consultant

This is THE Enneagram book everyone needs. It takes you on a journey where you uncover layers about yourself, one chapter at a time, and has something for everyone. Beginners will find it truly useful, and Enneagram experts will really indulge in the inner work invitation it offers. Ginger clearly used her decades of extensive work with the Enneagram to create a very rich and immersive experience for everyone who reads this book.

DEVELOPMENT BY DESIGN

The Enneagram and the Law of Three

Ginger Lapid-Bogda PhD

Development by Design
The Enneagram and The Law of Three

Copyright ©2026 by Ginger Lapid-Bogda PhD
All rights reserved. No portion of this book may be reproduced or transmitted in any form or by any means, electronic or mechanical, including photocopying, recording or by any information storage and retrieval system without the prior written permission of the author.

ISBN 979-8-9875540-7-4

The Enneagram in Business Press
Albany, California
510.570.2971

www.TheEnneagramInBusiness.com
©2026 Ginger Lapid-Bogda PhD

Dedicated to
Alice, Tze Meng, Granville, and the Enneagram
community in Singapore who
inspired this book

TABLE OF CONTENTS

Introduction to Development by Design — VII

PART 1
FOUNDATIONS

Introduction	2
Enneagram Types 1 – 9	3
What is my Enneagram Type?	21
Triangles, Centers of Intelligence, Wings, Arrows	22
Triads, Invisible Triangles	24
Instincts	26
Highlights	27

Introduction	29
General Self-Mastery	30
Self-Mastery Self-Assessment	31
Awareness Is NOT Consciousness	39
Psychological Assessment	40
Spiritual Assessment	44
True Self - False Self	48
Law of Three	59
Reflection	60
Highlights	61

PART 2
WHERE AM I NOW?

PART 3
WHAT AM I MOVING TOWARD?

Introduction	63
Law of Three Revisited	64
Somatic Power	65
The Importance of Imagination	66
Development Pathways	67
Enneagram as a Map	70
Awareness, Exploration and Practice	81
Awareness	82
Exploration	88
Practice	92
Highlights	94

TABLE OF CONTENTS

PART 4
WHAT AM I MOVING AGAINST?

Introduction	97
Three Forces of Transformation	98
11 Forms of Resistance	101
Shadow	105
Projection as Avoidance	107
Structure of Resistance	108
Shadow Work	119
Development Paths	128
Wings as Shadows	129
Highlights	130

PART 5
REACHING RECONCILIATION

Introduction	133
5 Attributes of the 3rd Force	134
True Self and Law of Three	135
Centers of Intelligence and Law of Three	138
Centers of Intelligence and Wholeness	140
Opening Your Centers	141
Integrating Your Centers through Music	150
Arrows, Triads	151
Freeing the Instincts	167
Subtype-Based Development	180
Catalytic Conversions through Subtypes	199
Create Your Mandala	200
Development Planning Process	203
Highlights	206

PART 6
BEYOND THE BOOK

The Book Creators	210
Beyond the Book Resources	211
Notes	213

INTRODUCTION

WHY I WROTE THIS BOOK

From my first exposure to the Enneagram 30+ years ago at a program led by Helen Palmer and after having written 10 Enneagram books and trained thousands of Enneagram professionals worldwide, the Enneagram's purpose has always been clear: *it is the development of individual and human consciousness.*

What is meant by development? It can mean many things, all good: growth, positive change, honest self-reflection, deep self-acceptance, less unnecessary suffering, and transformation. It can be psychological, spiritual or a combination of both. Development can be personal, professional and both simultaneously. All of these, however, require a relaxation of the human ego.

The Enneagram, more than any other system I know, targets the human ego directly and offers both insight and targeted development actions specific to the ego structure of each Enneagram type. It is a brilliant system for doing that in a respectful, effective, and stimulating way.

And that is the reason I have written this book. As someone who has traveled the globe with the Enneagram and was president of the International Enneagram Association over 20 years ago, I've seen a number of shifts in the Enneagram over the decades. Recently, there's been an explosion of interest in the Enneagram, along with the challenge of how to learn and use the Enneagram with accuracy and depth, especially in this era of mass media. There's also been a parallel interest from people who are already using the Enneagram and want to go both deeper and wider with it. This book is for everyone who wants to work with the Enneagram accurately and with integrity.

WHO THIS BOOK IS FOR

Are you an Enneagram teacher or trainer? Are you a coach, consultant, HR professional or a leader? Perhaps you're someone who loves the Enneagram and wants to explore the multiple opportunities it offers for development.

Then again, maybe you learned the Enneagram from a source where the Enneagram was taught more as a description of nine types with minimal focus on development.

Perhaps you learned that once you identified your Enneagram type, development mattered, but there was only one way or path for doing this.

You may be very new to the Enneagram, yet you are intrigued by it. I have said for decades that we don't find the Enneagram, it finds us when we are ready.

Perhaps you have worked with the Enneagram for decades and are looking for new ideas or a comprehensive framework for using the Enneagram for development.

This book is designed for all of you!

INTRODUCTION

ABOUT THIS BOOK'S ORIGINS

Is this a book, a workbook, an illustrated book, or all of the above?

The initial concept was to create a notebook as a companion to my newest Enneagram program, "Development by Design." The notebook was full of clear concepts and new ways of understanding the system and types. It began to tell a bigger story about development based on Gurdjieff's Law of Three or the three energies of change – the affirming 1st force, the denying 2nd force, and the reconciling 3rd force. It was clear this was no longer simply a workshop notebook; it was a book.

We love graphics that tell a conceptual story, and the more graphics we created, the more we wanted. Thus, the book became an illustrated book.

We also wanted to engage readers as fully as possible, so the illustrated book also became a workbook. You'll find self-assessments to complete and questions to reflect on and answer.

THE BOOK'S STRUCTURE

Part 1 Foundations provides an overview of the 9 Enneagram types along with specific aspects of the Enneagram system used as foundations for development throughout this book. These include the three Centers of Intelligence, wings, arrows, triads, and instincts.

Part 2 Where am I now? addresses this fundamental question because effective growth requires an accurate sense of your current development level. In addition to multiple self-assessments, you'll find information and activities to support your journey from false-self to true-self.

Parts 3-5 are each based on Gurdjieff's Law of Three, providing nuanced concepts and engaging development activities. These guide you in understanding how the three forces are operating in your chosen development area and fully integrated with insights from the Enneagram:

Part 3 What am I moving toward?
Affirming Force, 1st force - initiating energy

Part 4 What my I moving against?
Denying Force, 2nd force - opposing energy

Part 5 Where is the place of reconciliation?
Reconciling Force, 3rd force - harmonizing energy

In any process of creation or transformation, these three forces are always at play. Without all three forces, no real transformation can occur.

INTRODUCTION IX

Throughout, you'll see two symbols that indicate something specific:

 The avatar (which actually looks like me, Ginger) means please read this key concept because it provides the context for the activity that follows.

The pen indicates something for you to complete within the workbook itself.

GRATITUDE

Thanks to Gwen Baker-Yuill for partnering with me through her beautiful graphics and layout, to Alice Yuen and Tze Meng Chin for their ideas and feedback, and to Gail Barber, Tom Hattersley, and Pauline Towers-Dykeman for their detailed book edits. Additional gratitude to the Enneagram teachers who have influenced and inspired me most: Helen Palmer, Don Riso, and Claudio Naranjo.

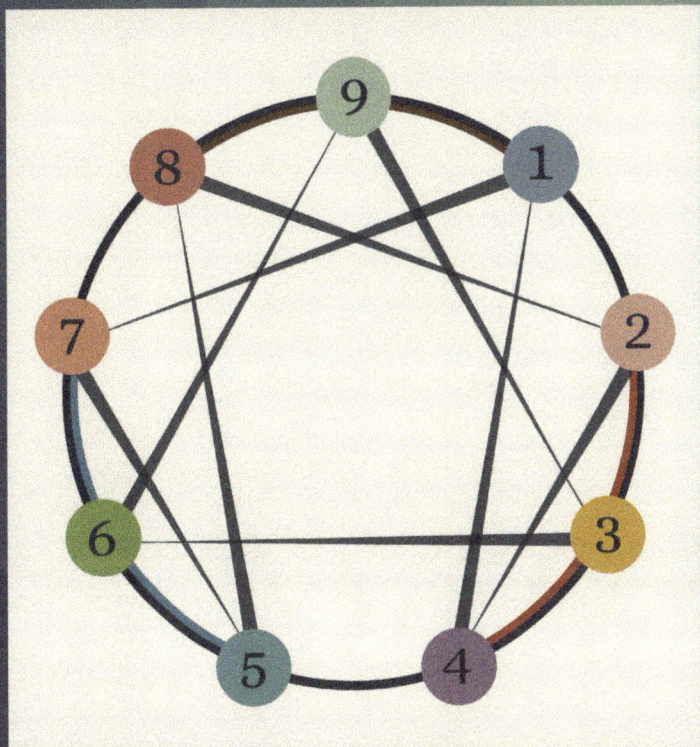

PART 1: FOUNDATIONS
TABLE OF CONTENTS

Introduction	2
Enneagram Types 1 – 9	3
What is my Enneagram Type?	21
Triangles, Centers of Intelligence, Wings, Arrows	22
Triads, Invisible Triangles	24
Instincts	26
Highlights	27

PART 1 FOUNDATIONS

INTRODUCTION

The Enneagram is an ancient system illuminating nine distinct ego structures or human archetypes. Each of the nine ego-structures has specific patterns of thinking, feeling and behaving. These patterns come to our attention through honest self-reflection and inquiry.

The nine types, reflected on the Enneagram symbol as numbers 1-9, come with characteristic strengths and development areas as well as development activities specific for that type. To use the Enneagram for transformative development, it is essential to identify your type accurately. You can read about each type on the following pages.

After the overview of the nine types, there's more information about the Enneagram system and specific configurations within the nine types that are particularly useful to your development. This is titled "triangles."

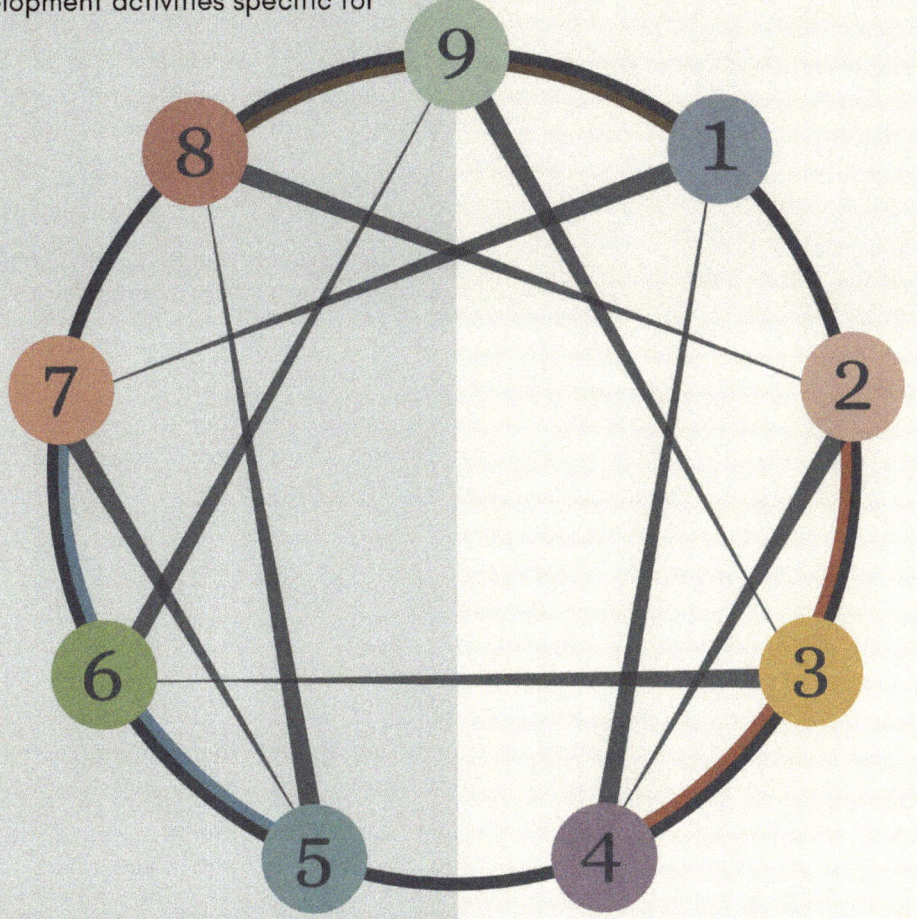

PART 1 FOUNDATIONS

TYPE ONE

Ones seek a perfect world and work diligently to improve both themselves and everyone and everything around them.

Strengths | strive for quality | organized | perceptive | honest
Development areas | reactive | critical | opinionated | impatient

Ones search for perfection and avoid making mistakes. Symbolized by this simple and elegant tree, Ones are rooted and grounded, upright in a variety of ways, and they are also prudent, self-controlled, and more structured than flexible.

Discerning and judging, quality-focused and responsible, organized and resentful, Enneagram Ones structure their worlds and exert self-control in order to ensure that they, others around them, and their environments align as closely as possible to their refined and precise ideals and standards of excellence. Ones don't really believe that true perfection is possible, but they do believe what matters most is that people are constantly working on improvement toward these ideals.

All Ones have an internalized set of high standards, a long series of expectations about how they and others should behave, as well as how activities should be structured and executed. All Ones, however, do not necessarily share the same exact standards. In addition, some Ones worry in advance about meeting their standards and getting everything right; some Ones perceive themselves as closer to perfect than the rest of us and view themselves as role models of excellence; and some Ones direct their standards of perfection to others by constantly trying to help others improve!

The One's interpersonal style is normally clear, precise, direct, and exacting, using carefully chosen words and phrases expressed in a seemingly polite manner. They are both disciplined and spontaneously reactive, amused and skeptical, playful and decidedly serious, and gracious, yet prone to flares of irritation or outbursts of anger.

While we can all be perfectionists at times, with high standards and a tendency to criticize both ourselves and others, for Ones, the search for perfection and the avoidance of mistakes are their primary, persistent, and driving motivations.

PART 1 FOUNDATIONS

TYPE ONE
ARE YOU A ONE?

If you answer Yes to three or four of these questions, you may be an Enneagram One.

1. Do you believe that if it's not worth doing right, it's not worth doing?
   ○ YES ○ NO ○ MAYBE

2. Do you think that there is almost always one right way to do things?
   ○ YES ○ NO ○ MAYBE

3. Do you think it's not OK to express anger, so you call it frustration, upset or irritation instead?
   ○ YES ○ NO ○ MAYBE

4. Do you have trouble delegating because you think no one can do it as correctly or as well as you?
   ○ YES ○ NO ○ MAYBE

Check out these core development suggestions for Ones. Are these your development areas, too?

Become accepting, calm, and serene rather than trying to make everything perfect
   ○ YES ○ NO ○ MAYBE

Let go of being overly attentive to details and needing to have everything under control
   ○ YES ○ NO ○ MAYBE

Become more flexible and relaxed and less judgmental and reactive
   ○ YES ○ NO ○ MAYBE

PART 1 FOUNDATIONS

TYPE TWO

Twos want to be liked by those they want to like them, try to meet the needs of others, and attempt to orchestrate the people and events in their lives.

Strengths | empathic | supportive | motivating | warm
Development areas | accommodating | indirect | angry when unappreciated | overextending

Twos search for appreciation and avoid feeling unworthy. Symbolized by this gift they can offer to others, Twos try to provide resources they believe the other person wants or needs: attention, time, an object the other admired, a poem or a kind word, advice, or even a surprise.

Optimistic, generous, and empathic, Enneagram Twos focus on the needs and behavior of others far more than on their own needs and desires; they develop an intuitive ability to know how to best support others in achieving their dreams or in minimizing their suffering. It isn't true that all Twos want everyone with whom they come in contact to like them. A more accurate understanding is that Twos want, and even expect, the people they want to like them to respond favorably, but care far less - if at all - whether people they dislike find them appealing. What is true of almost all Twos is that they can become extremely distressed when someone whose opinion or affection they care about perceives them in a negative way.

Most Twos appear warm, are good listeners, and offer advice that they hope and expect others will take. Some Twos appear vulnerable, even childlike, as if needing protection; other Twos exhibit more assertiveness, focusing their efforts to help or move groups or institutions in a forward direction; and other Twos derive their sense of value and importance by being desirable and indispensable to special individuals in their lives.

Twos tend to engage with others in a consistently warm way, usually asking questions of others more often than talking about themselves. While most Twos have well-developed interpersonal skills, they can also become self-effacing and uncomfortable when the focus is primarily on them.

While we can all be thoughtful and want others to think well of us, for Twos, the search for appreciation and the avoidance of feeling unworthy are their primary, persistent, and driving motivations.

PART 1 FOUNDATIONS

TYPE TWO
ARE YOU A TWO?

If you answer Yes to three or four of these questions, you may be an Enneagram Two.

1. Are relationships extremely important to you and always have been?
   - YES
   - NO
   - MAYBE

2. Are you really good at asking people questions about themselves as a way to get to know them better?
   - YES
   - NO
   - MAYBE

3. Do you continuously read other people's verbal and nonverbal communications and do this intuitively and accurately?
   - YES
   - NO
   - MAYBE

4. Are you an optimistic person, particularly when thinking about other people and their potential?
   - YES
   - NO
   - MAYBE

Check out these core development suggestions for Twos. Are these your development areas, too?

Acknowledge that you have needs and desires, and focus more on taking care of yourself and less on catering to the needs of others
   - YES
   - NO
   - MAYBE

Find an internal basis for self-esteem rather than making your self-worth dependent on the reactions of others
   - YES
   - NO
   - MAYBE

Integrate dependence and autonomy in both your personal and professional relationships
   - YES
   - NO
   - MAYBE

PART 1 FOUNDATIONS

TYPE THREE

Threes organize their lives to achieve specific goals and to appear successful in order to gain the respect and admiration of others.

Strengths | energetic | entrepreneurial | confident | results oriented
Development areas | competitive | abrupt | overly focused | selectively disclosing

Threes search for success and avoid failure at all costs. Symbolized by the target, Threes take steady aim at their goals, develop a plan for hitting the bulls-eye, and then do everything they can to hit their mark.

High energy, confident, and achievement-oriented, Enneagram Threes focus on goals they believe will bring them the respect of others and on efficient and effective plans for accomplishing these. As a result, Threes create a persona of confidence and success, but often at the expense of being completely genuine. They then lose touch with their deeper feelings and sense of who they really are, confusing their "public" image with their real selves.

Although all Threes share a success orientation and constant need to have goals and plans, there are also differences among them. Some Threes are highly self-reliant, strive to be the model of a "good" person, and create an image of being authentic and having no image; other Threes create an image of being high status, having prestige, and being important as a result of their ability to perform and their credentials, position, and high-influence friends; and some Threes focus more on creating an image of being extremely attractive in a highly masculine or feminine way, having less need for visibility and a greater desire to support the success of important people in their lives.

The Three's interpersonal style is one of having a convincing, deliberate, and confident stage presence. They convey their ideas in a well-conceived and highly self-assured way, have strong social skills except when they are stressed – at which times they can be cold and abrupt – and often appear as if they were born to give public presentations.

While we can all be results-oriented and have difficulty differentiating between what we do or how we try to appear and who we really are, for Threes, the search for success and the avoidance of failure are their primary, persistent, and driving motivations.

PART 1 FOUNDATIONS

TYPE THREE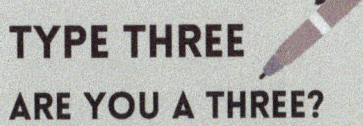

ARE YOU A THREE?

If you answer Yes to three or four of these questions, you may be an Enneagram Three.

1. Do you create goals and plans easily and feel lost if you don't have these?

   ○ YES   ○ NO   ○ MAYBE

2. Are you good at reading your audience and making adjustments as needed?

   ○ YES   ○ NO   ○ MAYBE

3. Do you believe your value comes from what you do and accomplish?

   ○ YES   ○ NO   ○ MAYBE

4. Do you focus on work and tasks and think that dealing with emotions for too long is a waste of time?

   ○ YES   ○ NO   ○ MAYBE

Check out these core development suggestions for Threes. Are these your development areas, too?

Deeply explore your inner thoughts, feelings, and experiences in order to become more genuine

   ○ YES   ○ NO   ○ MAYBE

Go more with the flow of events and experiences and be less driven to continuously try to make things happen

   ○ YES   ○ NO   ○ MAYBE

Learn the difference between doing and being, and value yourself for who you are rather than for what you do

   ○ YES   ○ NO   ○ MAYBE

PART 1 FOUNDATIONS

TYPE FOUR

Fours desire deep connections with their own inner worlds and with others and feel most alive when they authentically express their feelings and experiences.

Strengths | inspiring | creative | introspective | expressive
Development areas | intense | self-conscious | moody | guilt-ridden

Fours search for deep experiences and emotional connection and avoid rejection and feeling not-good-enough. Symbolized by the jigsaw puzzle piece, Fours perceive themselves as a puzzle, as they try to figure out why they feel so different from others and what makes them unique.

Individualistic, emotionally sensitive, and creative, Fours seek deep meaning, authentic connections, and they tend to idealize that which seems unavailable, being especially attuned to what is missing in their complex worlds. Focusing on their internal experiences as a way of understanding and finding meaning, Fours seek to be deeply understood and want to be perceived as unique, special, or different.

Although all Fours have a special connection to suffering and have robust, complex inner lives full of nuance and symbolism, some Fours are hyper-active and risk-taking, silently enduring their suffering as a badge of virtue; some Fours are hypersensitive and more despairing, wanting to be accepted unconditionally for who they are; and some Fours exhibit a flair for the dramatic and engage in extreme competition with others in hopes of winning and taking center-stage, thus minimizing their sense of not being good enough.

The Four's interpersonal style combines an abundance of self-referencing speech – that is, the extensive use of words such as *I*, *me*, *my*, and *mine* as well as personal stories – and they often use emotion-laden and metaphoric language. It is as if their own inner worlds are the center of the universe, or at least, the center of their universe.

While we can all suffer at times and almost everyone wants to be understood, for Fours, the search for deep experiences and connection and the avoidance of rejection or feeling not-good-enough are their primary, persistent, and driving motivations.

PART 1 FOUNDATIONS

TYPE FOUR

ARE YOU A FOUR?

If you answer Yes to three or four of these questions, you may be an Enneagram Four.

1. Do you think of yourself as original, one of a kind, so that no one is quite like you?
   ○ YES   ○ NO   ○ MAYBE

2. Are you introspective, and do you enjoy spending time exploring your inner world of thoughts and feelings?
   ○ YES   ○ NO   ○ MAYBE

3. Do you believe you are what you feel, even though your feelings change regularly?
   ○ YES   ○ NO   ○ MAYBE

4. Are you good at and enjoy helping others explore their feelings and experiences in great depth?
   ○ YES   ○ NO   ○ MAYBE

Check out these core development suggestions for Fours. Are these your development areas, too?

Integrate objectivity with emotionality to find an equilibrium of your heart and mind
   ○ YES   ○ NO   ○ MAYBE

Find a deep sense of self-worth without comparing yourself to others
   ○ YES   ○ NO   ○ MAYBE

Focus simultaneously and equally on yourself and other people
   ○ YES   ○ NO   ○ MAYBE

PART 1 FOUNDATIONS

TYPE FIVE

Fives thirst for information and knowledge and use emotional detachment as a way of keeping involvement with others to a minimum.

Strengths | analytic | objective | systematic | expert
Development areas | secretive | detached | autonomous | under-emphasize relationships

Fives search for knowledge and wisdom and avoid intrusion and loss of energy. Symbolized by the light bulb of mental knowledge, Fives try to accumulate information from which they can gain information and insight.

Emotionally detached, private, self-controlled, and highly independent, Fives have an insatiable need for information, particularly about areas that interest or concern them. This helps Fives believe that they are on the path to wisdom, but just as important, accumulating knowledge helps them feel prepared for the inevitable surprises they would prefer to avoid. Their quest for privacy is a constant, although not all Fives have the same areas they consider confidential.

All Fives automatically detach from their feelings in the actual moment, reactivating some of these later at a more private time. Fives also compartmentalize or isolate aspects of their lives from other parts – their work from their home life, their friends from each other, or themselves from other people.

Extremely wary of intrusions on their physical space, time and energy, some Fives keep extremely controlled boundaries and prefer seclusion; others are more social – though the content of their social conversations tends to be information, facts and values that interest them. Some Fives are highly self-disclosing and even emotional, but only with the few people they trust and have confidence in.

The Five's interpersonal style is highly self-contained, with minimal animation in either voice tone or body language. Some Fives may appear forthcoming about giving information, and others less so, but all Fives appear remote to some degree.

While we can all be emotionally detached and many people enjoy interesting information, for Fives, the search for knowledge and wisdom and the avoidance of intrusion and loss of energy are their primary, persistent, and driving motivations.

PART 1 FOUNDATIONS

TYPE FIVE
ARE YOU A FIVE?

If you answer Yes to three or four of these questions, you may be an Enneagram Five.

1. Do you guard your privacy closely, sharing information about yourself with only a few select people?

   ○ YES   ○ NO   ○ MAYBE

2. Is it important to you that people respect your personal space and do not sit or stand too close to you?

   ○ YES   ○ NO   ○ MAYBE

3. Do you not experience most feelings in real time, but actually process and reflect on them later when you are alone?

   ○ YES   ○ NO   ○ MAYBE

4. Do you believe logic is objective and trustworthy, but view emotions as too subjective?

   ○ YES   ○ NO   ○ MAYBE

Check out these core development suggestions for Fives. Are these your development areas, too?

Engage emotionally in real-time rather than automatically disengaging from your emotional responses

   ○ YES   ○ NO   ○ MAYBE

Share more of yourself — including your thoughts, feelings, and personal experiences — with others

   ○ YES   ○ NO   ○ MAYBE

Be a central part of events, interpersonal interactions, and organizations, rather than staying on the periphery

   ○ YES   ○ NO   ○ MAYBE

PART 1 FOUNDATIONS

TYPE SIX

Sixes are insightful, prone to worry, and create anticipatory scenarios in order to feel prepared if something goes wrong; some engage in risk to prove their fearlessness.

Strengths | loyal | collaborative | persevering | problem solving
Development areas | worrying | intolerance of ambiguity | analysis paralysis | martyring

Sixes search for meaning, certainty, and trust and try to avoid negative scenarios from occurring. Symbolized by the question mark inside the mind, Sixes question everything a way to prepare for all contingencies.

Sharp-minded, insightful, and loyal, Sixes are issue identifiers and problem solvers, with a mental-emotional antenna that is finely attuned to anticipate problems before they occur. This allows them to create multiple contingency paths in advance. Sixes are complex and run the gamut from phobic Sixes, who are overtly fearful, to counter-phobic Sixes, who mask their fears by taking dramatic risks. These challenges and risks, often physical ones, adrenalize them and prove to themselves and others that they are not fearful. Most Sixes display some characteristics of phobia and counter-phobia.

All Sixes worry as a habit of mind. Some worry constantly and are also warm, inviting, and good at creating safety through developing strong and loyal bonds with other people. Some Sixes become extraordinarily dutiful, wanting to know and adhere to the "rules" as a way to not get in trouble by going astray. Still other Sixes - the most counter-phobic of the Sixes - turn their fear into demonstrations of strength as a way to convince themselves and others of their bravery.

Sixes have a variety of interpersonal styles, but most are engaging, loyal, and lacking in pretentiousness. They tend to be candid, agile in expressing concerns, and willing to talk truthfully about themselves.

While we can all worry, be insightful, and want to feel well-prepared for the various scenarios life offers, for Sixes, the search for meaning, certainty, and trust, and the avoidance of negative scenarios from occurring are their primary, persistent, and driving motivations.

PART 1 FOUNDATIONS

TYPE SIX

ARE YOU A SIX?

If you answer Yes to three or four of these questions, you may be an Enneagram Six.

1. Do you like to think through various contingencies before you take action?
   ○ YES   ○ NO   ○ MAYBE

2. Do you calculate risk on an ongoing basis, being risk-avoidant, risk-approaching or both?
   ○ YES   ○ NO   ○ MAYBE

3. Do you have a very active mind that is hard to keep still and calm?
   ○ YES   ○ NO   ○ MAYBE

4. Are you a loyal and responsible person, particularly with those close to you or teams to which you belong?
   ○ YES   ○ NO   ○ MAYBE

Check out these core development suggestions for Sixes. Are these your development areas, too?

Learn to differentiate between an insight and a projection (something based on imagination)
   ○ YES   ○ NO   ○ MAYBE

Trust your own inner authority rather than looking to someone or something outside yourself for meaning and certainty
   ○ YES   ○ NO   ○ MAYBE

Have faith in yourself and others to be able to handle whatever occurs
   ○ YES   ○ NO   ○ MAYBE

PART 1 FOUNDATIONS

TYPE SEVEN

Sevens crave stimulation from new ideas, people, and experiences, avoid pain, and engage in positive possibility planning in order to keep all of their options open.

Strengths | imaginative | enthusiastic | engaging | quick thinking
Development areas | impulsive | unfocused | rebellious | pain avoidant

Sevens search for pleasure and stimulation and avoid pain and discomfort. Symbolized by the glass of champagne, Sevens are bubbly and effervescent, trying to enjoy life's pleasures and positive possibilities.

Spontaneous, engaging, and multitasking to an extreme, Sevens are upbeat, energetic, and need to feel that they have all options possible open to them. Elaborate future planners, dreamers and visionaries, Sevens generate enthusiasm, push boundaries, and avoid painful experiences by creating new ideas, engaging with people or activities that excite them, and by rationalizing negative experiences through a positive reframing of events.

Almost all Sevens have difficulty focusing on one thing at a time, as their attention shifts from one idea, activity, or person to the next thing that grabs their interest. They also have a contagious sense of optimism that comes from a sense that everything is possible. Some Sevens create extensive social networks, a kind of collective surrogate family that they believe gives them the support to make the best of every opportunity; other Sevens restrain their desire to have everything as a way to sacrifice themselves in the service of the group; and still other Sevens are unabashed dreamers, looking to everything new to stimulate and excite them.

Their interpersonal style can be described as fast-talking and even faster thinking, with a mental process that moves 1000 miles per hour and jumps from topic to topic. While some Sevens are quiet, most Sevens say what's on their minds as soon as they think it. And although their ideas may seem loosely connected to the rest of us, Sevens make these associative connections instantly and share them in rapid fire, using voices filled with enthusiasm and energy.

While we can all be creative thinkers, enjoy the waves of dopamine, and prefer pleasure to pain, for Sevens, the search for pleasure and stimulation and the avoidance of pain and discomfort are their primary, persistent, and driving motivations.

PART 1 **FOUNDATIONS**   16

TYPE SEVEN
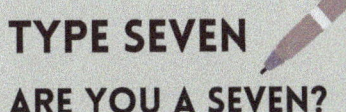
ARE YOU A SEVEN?

If you answer Yes to three or four of these questions, you may be an Enneagram Seven.

1. Do you think that being positive is always a choice and so you choose to be positive at almost all times?

   ○ YES   ○ NO   ○ MAYBE

2. Do you get feedback from others that they feel interrupted by you when you are actually saying something because you are excited by an idea?

   ○ YES   ○ NO   ○ MAYBE

3. Do you believe nobody has the right to restrict or limit you?

   ○ YES   ○ NO   ○ MAYBE

4. Is it hard for you to stay with your emotions for long periods of time, especially sadness and fear?

   ○ YES   ○ NO   ○ MAYBE

Check out these core development suggestions for Sevens. Are these your development areas, too?

Be able to focus mentally, emotionally, and physically at will

   ○ YES   ○ NO   ○ MAYBE

Feel genuine and consistent empathy for others

   ○ YES   ○ NO   ○ MAYBE

Accept and integrate the reality of pain and discomfort along with pleasure

   ○ YES   ○ NO   ○ MAYBE

PART 1 FOUNDATIONS

TYPE EIGHT

Eights pursue truth and justice, like to keep situations under control, want to make important things happen, and try to hide their vulnerability.

Strengths | direct | strategic | protective | big-action oriented
Development areas | controlling | demanding | disdain weakness | intimidating

Eights search for control and justice and avoid feeling vulnerable or weak. Symbolized by the mountain, Eights are solid and often immovable, strong, and difficult to penetrate.

Assertive, bold, and confident, Eights are highly independent, with a tendency to both protect and control people and events around them and a deep commitment to truth, justice, and equity or fairness. Most Eights are excessive in some way, particularly when they feel anxious or vulnerable. They strongly prefer to not show this side of themselves to others, perceiving such feelings as signaling weakness. Eights mask their tender side by engaging in excessiveness in a variety of forms: over-work, too much or too little exercise, erratic or unhealthy eating, and other forms of over-consumption, such as incessant shopping or the purchasing of items – often expensive ones – that they don't really need.

Eights want to get their needs and desires met, want to make big things happen quickly, much akin to moving mountains, and most have a big presence even when they are saying little. Eights can also appear somewhat different from one another. Some Eights are quiet with a low threshold for frustration and an ability to survive and gain control in almost any situation; other Eights are social rebels and protective of others to an extreme; and some Eights are highly emotional, extraordinarily passionate, and enjoy being more center stage.

The Eight's interpersonal style is assertive, and they use voice modulation and non-verbal behavior for effect and impact. For example, they may use a strident voice, direct eye contact, and move closer to others as a way to take charge or make their point. By contrast, they may use a softer voice tone, warm eye contact, and a smile to appear gracious, hospitable, or non-threatening.

While we can all highly value truth-telling and pursue justice, want to make big things happen, and have issues with not appearing weak, for Eights, the search for control and justice and the avoidance of vulnerability are their primary, persistent, and driving motivations.

PART 1 FOUNDATIONS

TYPE EIGHT
ARE YOU AN EIGHT?

If you answer Yes to three or four of these questions, you may be an Enneagram Eight.

1. Do you think that bigger is better, both in thought and action, as long as it is also strategic?
   ○ YES   ○ NO   ○ MAYBE

2. Are you a direct and assertive person who can intimidate people even when this may not be your intention?
   ○ YES   ○ NO   ○ MAYBE

3. Do you trust your 'gut' responses in almost everything you decide or do?
   ○ YES   ○ NO   ○ MAYBE

4. Do you have a bold exterior and have a difficult time showing your vulnerable side to others?
   ○ YES   ○ NO   ○ MAYBE

Check out these core development suggestions for Eights. Are these your development areas, too?

Be forthcoming about your deep vulnerabilities
   ○ YES   ○ NO   ○ MAYBE

Allow others to exercise autonomy and control
   ○ YES   ○ NO   ○ MAYBE

Be receptive and responsive to input from others rather than moving to immediate, unilateral action
   ○ YES   ○ NO   ○ MAYBE

PART 1 FOUNDATIONS

TYPE NINE

Nines seek peace, harmony, and positive mutual regard and dislike conflict, tension, demands, and ill will.

Strengths | diplomatic | easygoing | accepting | affable

Development areas | conflict avoidant | unassertive | procrastinating | indecisive

Nines search for harmony and comfort and avoid tension and conflict. Symbolized by the yin-yang symbol, they try to reconcile oppositional ideas, forces, and perspectives as a way to show respect for and integrate all sides.

Relaxed, easy to relate to, and accepting, Nines are usually excellent facilitators, drawing out the ideas of others so everyone gets heard. While they value harmony, seek comfortable ways of relating, and are adept mediators of conflict between others, Nines are extremely uncomfortable with conflict when they are directly involved. They refrain from doing things that could generate tension, such as not expressing opinions that could cause discord, and diffusing their attention rather than focusing on their own priorities. Nines may watch television for hours, work relentlessly, lose themselves on the internet, or just take a nap. They do this to avoid both having difficult conversations and having to do something they don't feel like doing.

Nines appear easygoing on the outside, but inside, there can be internal turmoil. Some Nines reduce this tension through satisfying their physical needs: eating, sleeping, and/or reading. Some Nines submerge themselves by working extraordinary hours in the service of groups. Some Nines find comfort in merging with another person and losing themselves in the process.

Their interpersonal style is agreeable and non-assertive, with an ability to discuss a variety of topics. Nines often nod their heads affirmatively, which doesn't mean they agree; it means they are listening to what is being said. Affable and humorous, they express themselves indirectly as a way to maintain positive relationships and minimize discord.

While we can all prefer rapport and ease to discord, for Nines, the search for harmony and comfort and the avoidance of conflict are their primary, persistent, and driving motivations.

PART 1   **FOUNDATIONS**   20

TYPE NINE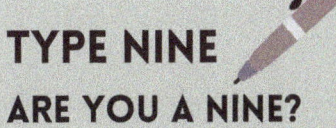
ARE YOU A NINE?

If you answer Yes to three or four of these questions, you may be an Enneagram Nine.

1. Do you wish that everyone could live in a world of mutual respect, minimal tension, and limited conflict?

   ○ YES   ○ NO   ○ MAYBE

2. Do you have trouble knowing and expressing what you do want, but are better at knowing what you don't want?

   ○ YES   ○ NO   ○ MAYBE

3. Do people tell you that you are highly approachable and very easy to talk to?

   ○ YES   ○ NO   ○ MAYBE

4. Do you dislike pressure to have to do something and find yourself saying 'yes' rather than 'no,' as a way to keep the peace?

   ○ YES   ○ NO   ○ MAYBE

Check out these core development suggestions for Nines. Are these your development areas, too?

Express your thoughts, needs, and preferences even when these oppose the wishes of others

   ○ YES   ○ NO   ○ MAYBE

Be active and assertive rather than acting de-energized and passive

   ○ YES   ○ NO   ○ MAYBE

Learn to embrace conflict and deal with it directly, with the understanding that resolving differences brings people together

   ○ YES   ○ NO   ○ MAYBE

PART 1 FOUNDATIONS

WHAT IS MY ENNEAGRAM TYPE?

If you don't already know your Enneagram type, now is a good time to do some preliminary thinking about this. Please remember that your type refers to your patterns of responses over time, not just how you perceive yourself in more recent times.

STEP 1: TYPE DESCRIPTIONS
Start by reflecting on what you read about each Enneagram type.

STEP 2: WHICH TYPE DESCRIPTIONS SOUNDED LIKE THEY COULD BE YOU?

Which type descriptions sound like they could be you?

Which type descriptions did not sound like you at all?

Which types are a maybe?

Use your responses above to compare to your answers to the four questions summary below.

STEP 4: FOUR QUESTIONS
Now, review your answers to the four questions for each type.

Which types received 3-4 yesses?

Which types were mostly nos?

Which types were maybes?

STEP 5: YOUR LIKELY TYPE
Your Enneagram type is most likely among the types that received 3-4 yesses. Consider these as top choices, compare them to the types you selected from reading the type descriptions, and answer these questions:

What is your most likely Enneagram type?

What might be other viable possibilities?

PART 1 FOUNDATIONS

TRIANGLES

The Enneagram is comprised of multiple triangles. Here are several triangles especially useful for development (see Part 5 of this book).

CENTERS OF INTELLIGENCE

The concept of Centers of Intelligence is foundational to understanding the Enneagram system and the 9 types. First, three Enneagram types are formed in each Center of Intelligence and, as a result, share a similar focus and common emotion. Second, a core purpose of the Enneagram is to become more whole, and one path to wholeness involves increasing our access to the productive use of each of the three Centers. The Enneagram type provides a roadmap of insight into how each Enneagram type productively uses and misuses each of these three Centers.

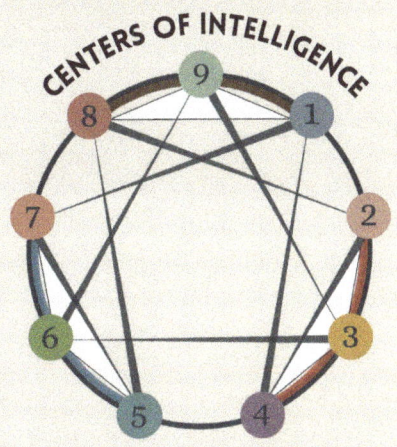

Head Center triangle 5 – 6 – 7
- Focus: Thinking, security, anxiety
- Common emotion: fear

Heart Center triangle 2 – 3 – 4
- Focus: Feelings, image, approval
- Common emotion: sorrow

Body Center Triangle 8 – 9 – 1
- Focus: Instinct, justice, control
- Common emotion: anger

Transformation begins by increasing conscious access to all three Centers:

Head
Clarity, perspective, vision

Heart
Empathy, resonance, emotional truth

Body
Groundedness, somatic intelligence, right action

Access is about opening these three channels and using them in an integrated way, not forcing a "balance" among or between them.

PART 1 FOUNDATIONS

WINGS

Wings are the Enneagram types on each side of your core Enneagram type. These are secondary types of your core type, which means that you may also display some of the characteristics of these Enneagram types. Wings do not fundamentally change your Enneagram type; they merely offer you resources and additional qualities. As can be seen on the Enneagram symbol, Nine and Two are wings for Ones, One and Three are wings for Twos, Two and Four are wings for Threes, and so forth.

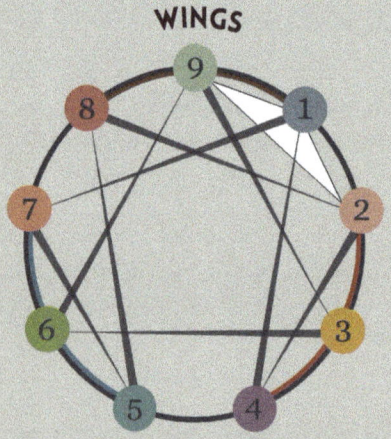

You may have one wing, two wings, or no wings at all. It is also possible to have had one wing be more active when you were younger, and to have had the other appear as you matured. People of the same Enneagram type and identical wings may use their wing qualities differently.

It can be helpful to think of the two types on either side of our core type as energies that offer potential resources to us as we navigate our worlds.

ARROWS

Arrow lines refer to the two types on the Enneagram symbol that have an arrow pointing away from or toward your core Enneagram type, and you may show some characteristics of one or both of these two additional types. As can be seen on the Enneagram symbol with the arrow tips added below, Two and Five are arrow lines for Eights. Five and One are arrow lines for Sevens, and so forth.

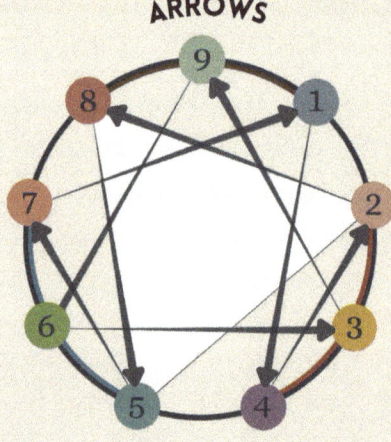

Access to your arrow lines can be beneficial, giving you additional complexity, nuance, and flexibility, but they do not change your fundamental type – that is, your patterns of thinking and feeling and motivational structure remain the same. You may have strong links to one arrow number, both arrow numbers, or neither arrow number. People of the same Enneagram type who have strong links to their arrow numbers may use these arrow qualities quite differently.

PART 1 FOUNDATIONS

TRIADS

There are several triads or groupings of three on the Enneagram. These include the optimistic triad (7, 9 and 2), the competency triad (1, 3 and 5) and the intensity triad (4, 6 and 8).

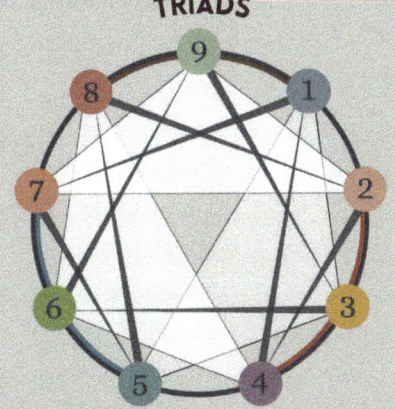

TRIADS

OPTIMISTIC TRIAD
TYPES 7, 9 AND 2

The three types in the optimistic triad, also called the positive outlook trio, have a positive overlay on reality so that the world looks better than it actually is. 7s are the most optimistic, taking a positive view of just about everything. 9s are moderately optimistic, perceiving people and events as generally positive. Finally, 2s try to see the best in other people – that is, until they don't! Although the three types within this trio are very different, people can get confused between and among them.

COMPETENCY TRIAD
TYPES 1, 3 AND 5

These three types want to both experience themselves as highly competent and be treated by others as highly competent, although competency means something different to each of these types. For 1s, competency means being right, knowing how to organize the best way, and having the most correct opinion. For 3s, competency means knowing how and being able to move things forward, being able to get great results, and understanding something they think they should know. For 5s, it means being competent in terms of their knowledge and knowing how things fit together. An exploration of what competency means helps sort out differences between these three types.

INTENSITY TRIAD
TYPES 4, 6 AND 8

Types 4, 6 and 8 are the most intense of the nine Enneagram types. Their intensity, however, comes from different sources. The 4s' intensity is emotional, a result of their many feelings playing and replaying internally and their drive for intense, authentic interactions. The 6s' intensity is the result of their ever-active minds playing and replaying various scenarios. The 8s' intensity is more somatic and comes from the body. It is often noted that people can feel the intense presence of 8s, even when they are saying absolutely nothing. Intensity is a very strong energy that these three types share, so that discerning the source of the intensity can be a key factor in differentiating between and among these types.

PART 1 FOUNDATIONS

INVISIBLE TRIANGLES
OBJECT RELATIONS TRIADS

The invisible triangles are often called the object relations triads. They describe the connection between our early relational experiences and our types.

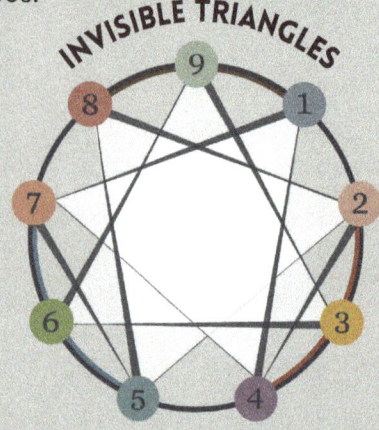

3-6-9: THE ATTACHMENT TRIAD
Relational Pattern
Attachment and Reassurance

These types struggle with losing connection and seek stability, approval, or certainty in relationships or structures.

- Type 3 - Attaches to success and image in search of approval
- Type 6 - Attaches to authority or beliefs in search of safety
- Type 9 - Attaches to comfort and routine in search of harmony

1-4-7: THE FRUSTRATION TRIAD
Relational Pattern
Frustration and Idealization

These types are disappointed when reality doesn't meet internal ideals and react with withdrawal, criticism, or escape.

- Type 1 - Frustrated by imperfection, seeks constant improvement
- Type 4 - Frustrated by lack of depth or uniqueness, longs for idealized deep connection
- Type 7 - Frustrated by limitation, craves variety, stimulation and joy

2-5-8: THE REJECTION TRIAD
Relational Pattern
Rejection and Autonomy

These types manage vulnerability by rejecting first, pushing others away, and withdrawing to maintain control.

- Type 2 - Fears rejection, seeks worthiness through giving, but rejects their own needs
- Type 5 - Fears intrusion and abandonment, retreats into their mind, rejecting emotional demands and connectivity
- Type 8 - Fears betrayal and lack of control, rejects vulnerability in self and others

INSTINCTS

Three basic human instincts create our needs and drive our behavior: self-preservation, social and one-to-one. The self-preservation instinct orients toward physical experience and issues of safety, security, danger, resources, structure, and control. The social instinct's focus is on belonging, community, groups, social relationships, and influence. The one-to-one instinct's emphasis is on intimacy, affection, relations with one other person, bonding, and attraction.

Instincts, by themselves, are inherently neither positive nor negative. They are simply three arenas in which we try to get our needs met. However, when our Enneagram type-based emotional pattern, called passion, mixes with one or more of our basic instincts, our instinctual needs become distorted by the passions. Each Enneagram type has a specific passion: Ones (anger): Twos (pride); Threes (deceit); Fours (envy); Fives (avarice); Sixes (fear); Sevens (gluttony); Eights (lust): and Nines (laziness).

This mix of instinct and type-based passion creates three versions of each type, called subtypes. The three subtypes of each type can appear very similar to each other - as in Enneagram Fives - or they can appear very different - for example, Enneagram Sixes.

PART 1 FOUNDATIONS

PART 1 HIGHLIGHTS

REMEMBER

Enneagram type is about patterns over a lifetime

No type is better than any other type

Accurate type identification opens transformational doors

DO'S

Take your time discovering your type
Be curious
Explore the whys, not the whats

DONT'S

Type other people unless you are trained
Try to be a type you are not
Be judgmental about any type

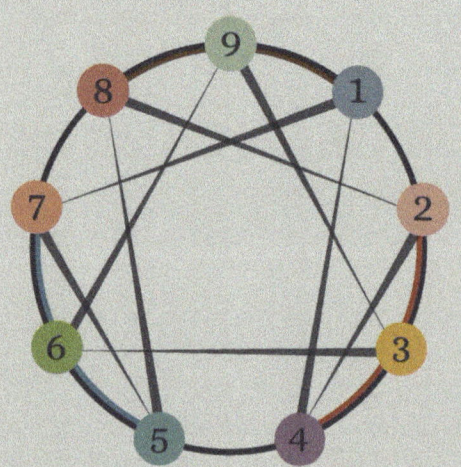

REFLECTIONS

"Honesty is the first chapter in the book of wisdom."
- Thomas Jefferson

"The privilege of a lifetime is to become who you truly are."
- Carl Jung

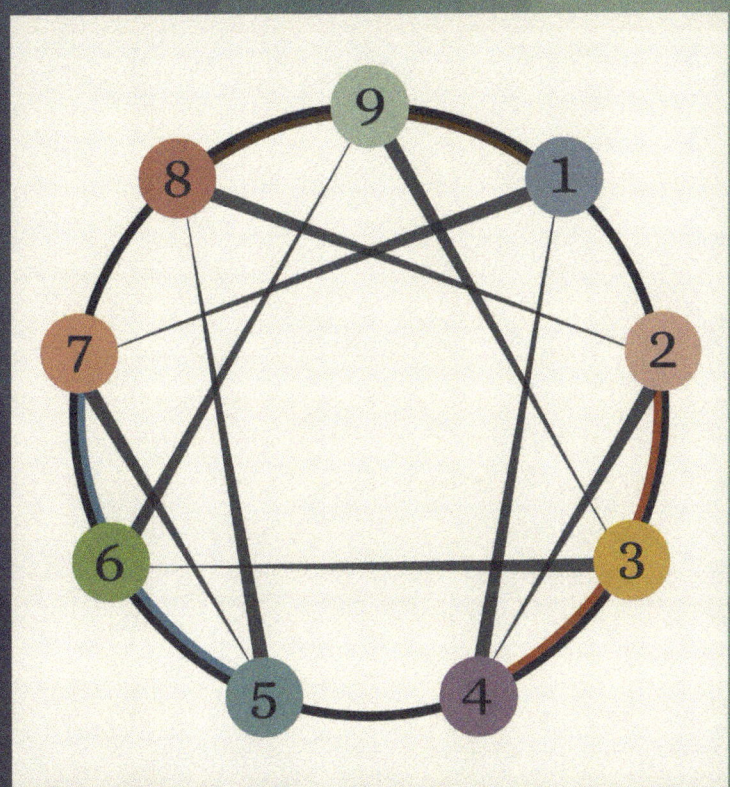

PART 2: WHERE AM I NOW?

TABLE OF CONTENTS

Introduction	29
General Self-Mastery	30
Self-Mastery Self-Assessment	31
Awareness Is NOT Consciousness	39
Psychological Assessment	40
Spiritual Assessment	44
True Self - False Self	48
Law of Three	59
Reflection	60
Highlights	61

INTRODUCTION

What do shopping malls, Disneyland, hiking trails, and car trips have in common? They all require us to know our "starting point" before we choose our path to our final destination. The development journey is no different!

Part 2 moves from knowing your Enneagram type in Part 1 to helping you identify your development journey's "starting point" through multiple self-assessments - general self-mastery and Enneagram type-specific self-mastery, followed by a psychological self-assessment and a spiritual self-assessment.

Perspective is crucial throughout the journey from "False Self" to "True Self." For this reason, information is provided about the distinction between these two selves and how the energetic forces of the Law of Three - affirming, denying, and reconciling - support our transformation from False Self to True Self.

PART 2 WHERE AM I NOW?

GENERAL SELF-MASTERY

Foundational to our development is an objective and honest assessment of our current self-mastery level so we can focus our development journey in productive and realistic ways. If we think we are more developed than we actually are, we won't be working toward true self-improvement. If we think we are less developed than is the case, we need to be more realistic so we don't focus on areas we have already developed.

But what is self-mastery? Here are the 9 components, all of which depend on self-awareness as a foundation.

Self-awareness | accurate identification of thoughts, feelings and behaviors, motivations, inner drives, and one's impact on others in the context of patterns, not isolated events

Responsive to feedback | engages feedback with the ability to discern what is accurate and what is not

Self-responsibility | takes responsibility, does not blame others, has a strong sense of agency

Self-motivation | an intrinsic, positive motivational structure, not motivated by external rewards or fear

Self-management | makes conscious choices rather than trying to under- or over-control reactions

Emotional maturity | makes wise and thoughtful choices, no matter what age

Personal vision | strong sense of purpose addressing the question "Why am I here?"

Integrity | productive behavior consistent with positive core values

Personality integration | access to head, heart, and the wisdom of the body

Lifelong learning commitment | continuously engaged in self-development

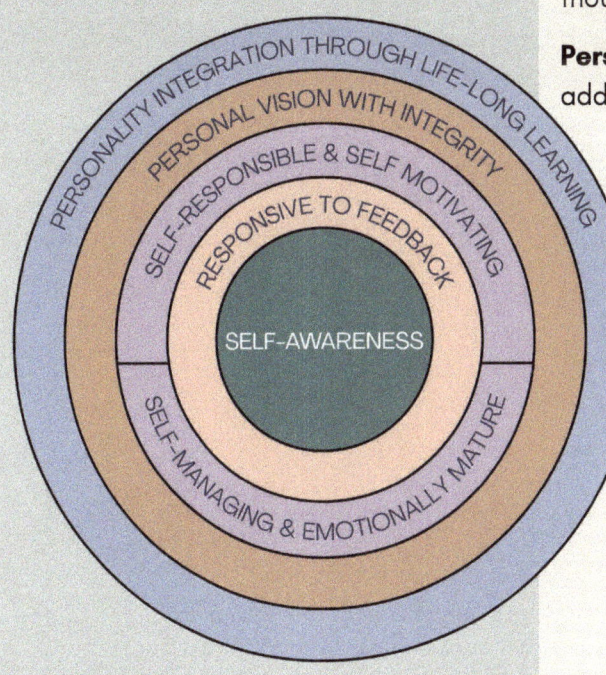

PART 2 WHERE AM I NOW?

SELF-MASTERY SELF-ASSESSMENT

DIRECTIONS

This is your opportunity to assess your overall level of self-mastery using these 10 self-mastery components. On the following page, fill in the circle under each factor that best describes your self-mastery on a normal or average day. Next, place an X in the circle under each factor that describes you when you are functioning below or less than normal for you. Then, place an X in the circle under each factor that describes you when you are functioning much higher than normal. These two Xs indicate your range for each factor: your lowest and highest.

Finally, take a ruler or straight edge and drawn a line between the lower ranges for each factor, the circle or average for each factor and the high Xs for each factor.

This will give you a visual graph of your overall self-mastery.

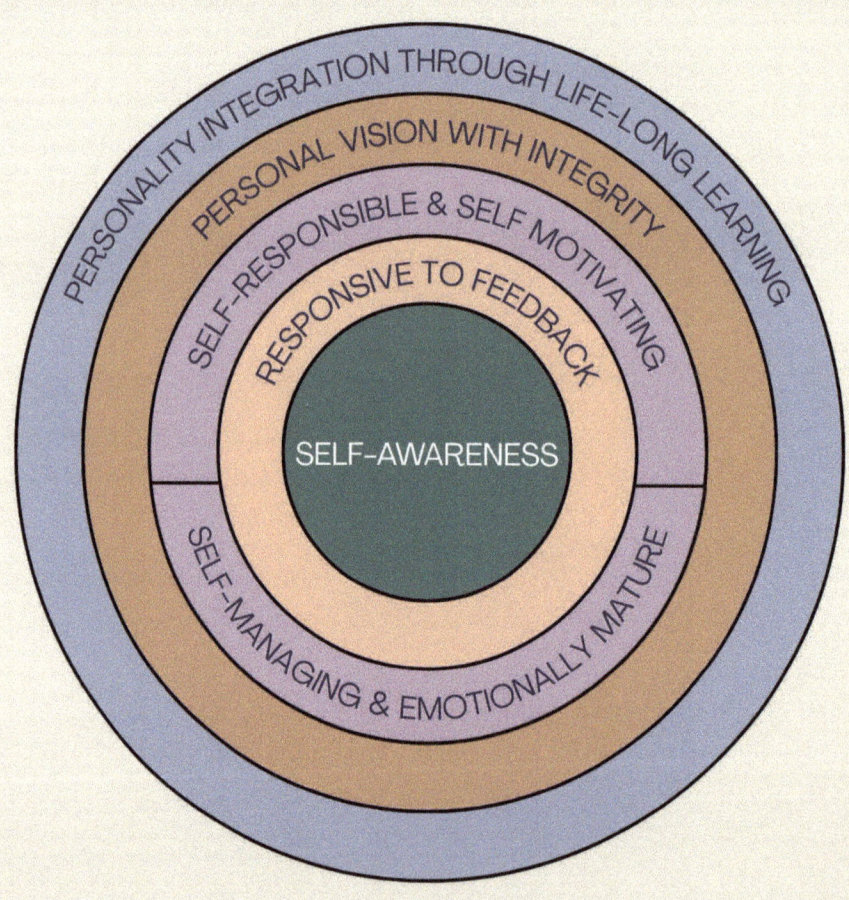

PART 2 WHERE AM I NOW?

Self-awareness | demonstrates a deep level of self-awareness of thoughts, feelings and behaviors, as well as of motivations, inner drives, and impact on others

LOW — MEDIUM — HIGH

Responsive to feedback | able to utilize accurate and useful feedback without this being contingent on who gives the feedback or the elegance of its delivery

LOW — MEDIUM — HIGH

Self-responsibility | takes full responsibility for own thoughts, feelings, and behaviors and does not blame others

LOW — MEDIUM — HIGH

Self-motivation | has an internal and positive motivational structure rather than being motivated by external sources or by fear

LOW — MEDIUM — HIGH

Self-management | makes conscious choices about own thoughts, feelings and behaviors rather than trying to under- or over-control reactions

LOW — MEDIUM — HIGH

Emotional maturity | chooses wisely and thoughtfully and integrates perspectives different from one's own

LOW — MEDIUM — HIGH

Personal vision | possesses a strong sense of purpose based on positive values

LOW — MEDIUM — HIGH

Integrity | exhibits productive behavior consistent with core values

LOW — MEDIUM — HIGH

Personality integration | has open access to head, heart, and body and uses them in an aligned way

LOW — MEDIUM — HIGH

Lifelong learning commitment | continuously engages in self-development

LOW — MEDIUM — HIGH

PART 2 WHERE AM I NOW?

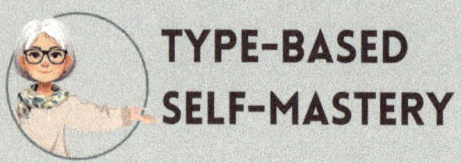

TYPE-BASED SELF-MASTERY

Why do people of the same type often appear and behave so differently? Although there are many reasons for this - age, culture, gender, subtypes - variations in self-mastery levels explain many of these differences. A type-specific description of self-mastery can give deeper insights into self-mastery levels. In the context of Enneagram type, self-mastery falls into three levels: low, which is fear-based; medium, which is concern-based; and high, which is based on a higher-level understanding.

TYPE-BASED SELF-MASTERY ASSESSMENT

DIRECTIONS

Doing an honest self-assessment contributes to your development so you know where you are and where to grow. Start by going to your Enneagram type and reading the descriptions for the three self-mastery levels for your type. Which self-mastery level for your Enneagram type best describes you? To be even more specific, under type with the three self-mastery levels, there are nine circles. Fill in the circle that describes you as you are now.

HIGH
Understanding based

MEDIUM
Concern based

LOW
Fear based

PART 2 WHERE AM I NOW?

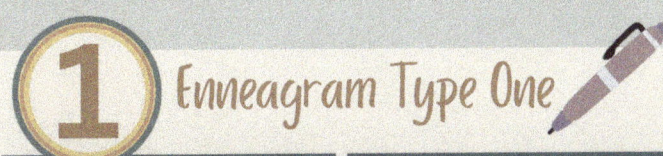

Enneagram Type One

Low Self-Mastery The Judge	Medium Self-Mastery The Teacher	High Self-Mastery The Serene Accepter
Core Fear Being bad or malevolent, having something deeply, intrinsically wrong with them	**Core Concern** Making mistakes, being imperfect	**Core Understanding** Everything, including imperfection, is just as it should be
Intolerant, tightly wound, inflexible, volatile, unstable, punishing, highly judgmental, unforgiving of self and others	Discerning, judging, opinionated, well-organized, methodical, wry, easily irritated, resentful, enamored of excellence in others, deeply dislike errors	Able to understand and diminish negative impact of inner critic, dignified, patient, accepting, astute self-observers, can be light-hearted and spontaneous

LOW — MEDIUM — HIGH

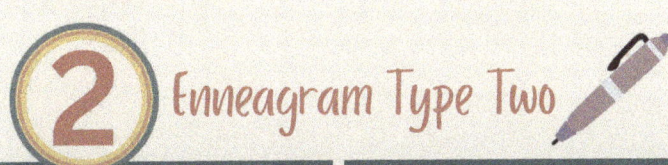

Enneagram Type Two

Low Self-Mastery The Manipulator	Medium Self-Mastery The Friend	High Self-Mastery The Humble Servant
Core Fear Being unwanted, discarded, and intrinsically unworthy	**Core Concern** Feeling valuable, liked, needed, appreciated and worthy	**Core Understanding** There is a profound purpose to everything that occurs that is independent of their own efforts
Master manipulators, using guilt and shame or blame to control, make others feel guilty and responsible for their unhappiness, aggressive, use full force to get what they want, take no responsibility for own behavior	Warm, with many friends, often at center of social circles, intuitive, read others well, engage through compliments, giving attention, asking questions or offering advice, emotional, hovering, difficulty saying no	No longer give to others as a way to bolster their own self-esteem, don't adapt or behave so that others will like them, deeply gentle, truly humble, inclusive, compassionate, emanate inner well-being

LOW — MEDIUM — HIGH

PART 2 WHERE AM I NOW?

Enneagram Type Three

Low Self-Mastery The Calculator	Medium Self-Mastery The Star	High Self-Mastery The Believer
Core Fear Extreme fear of failure, since failure would make them feel that they have no value	**Core Concern** Feeling successful, avoiding failure and gaining the respect of others	**Core Understanding** Everyone has intrinsic value, and there is a natural flow and order to everything
Insincere, self-serving, opportunistic, pursue what they want with minimal regard for others, isolated, hide inner emptiness, aggressive and defensive when image or façade is challenged	Over-focus on goals and plans, driven, competitive, seek recognition, motivated primarily by success, not always authentic, wonder who they really are aside from accomplishments	Know who they are separate from what they do or the roles they play, know what they feel, admit their insecurities, contagious enthusiasm, genuine, spontaneous, able to go with the natural flow

LOW — MEDIUM — HIGH

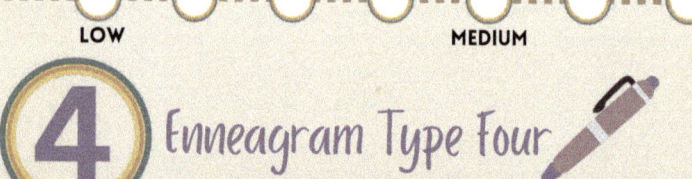

Enneagram Type Four

Low Self-Mastery The Invisible Defective	Medium Self-Mastery The Unique Individual	High Self-Mastery The Appreciator
Core Fear Being intrinsically defective and completely disconnected	**Core Concern** Feeling significant, feeling special and finding meaning	**Core Understanding** Everything has meaning and significance, and everyone is connected at the deepest levels
Bitter, depressed, emotionally volatile, hypersensitive, self-absorbed, highly sensitive to rejection, deeply ashamed, alienated, rageful, withdrawn and/or highly aggressive	Dramatic or reticent, seek meaning through authenticity, imaginative, self-expressive, self-referencing, prolonged personal storytelling, compare self to others, moody, melancholic, empathic	Centered, tranquil, universal artistic expression, grateful, graceful, whole, consistent, gently empathic, true concern for others, do not engage in emotional turmoil

LOW — MEDIUM — HIGH

PART 2 WHERE AM I NOW?

5 Enneagram Type Five

Low Self-Mastery The Fearful Strategist	Medium Self-Mastery The Remote Expert	High Self-Mastery The Integrated Wizard
Core Fear Being helpless, incapable, depleted and overtaken	**Core Concern** Scarce resources and energy, privacy, and competence through knowledge	**Core Understanding** Wisdom involves integrating thoughts, feelings and action, based on direct experience
Frightened, withdrawn, isolated, hostile, believe others plan to do them harm, plot ways to circumvent danger, secretive, implosive, remove selves from interaction, extremely limited access to own feelings	Remote, private, guard time, energy, and autonomy, dislike surprises, reveal limited personal information, detach from feelings, keep needs minimal, independent, self-contained, spontaneous only with those they trust	Experience feelings in the moment, fully engage in life, lively, spontaneous, joyful, imaginative, fully integrate head, heart, and body, contagious zest for ideas, feelings, and experiences

LOW — MEDIUM — HIGH

6 Enneagram Type Six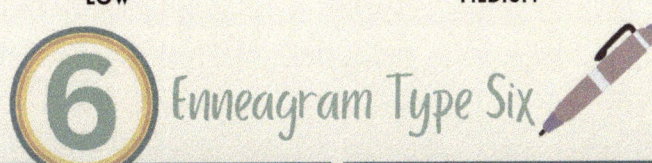

Low Self-Mastery The Coward	Medium Self-Mastery The Loyalist	High Self-Mastery The Courageous One
Core Fear Having no support or sense of meaning and being unable to survive	**Core Concern** Safety, belonging and being able to trust	**Core Understanding** Meaning and support exist both inside and outside themselves
Anxious, frenzied, engage in constant worst-case scenario development, project onto others, paranoid, increasingly clingy, dependent, panicky, punitive, reject those who disagree with them	Insightful, overly busy, approval seeking, focus on authority, reactive, alternate between trust and distrust, doubtful, confused, seek safety in cohesive groups, loyal to friends, groups, and leaders they trust	Intellectual, insightful, confident, calm, resilient, clear, courageous, trust own inner authority, connect with people in a deep, steady, and warmhearted way, clear-headed

LOW — MEDIUM — HIGH

PART 2 WHERE AM I NOW?

7 Enneagram Type Seven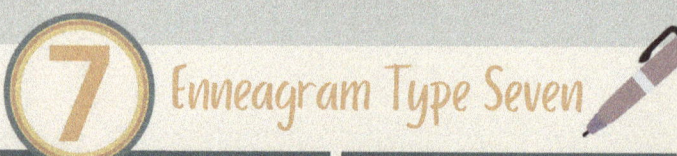

Low Self-Mastery The Frenetic Escape Artist	Medium Self-Mastery The Stimulator	High Self-Mastery The Focused Inspirer
Core Fear Pain, deprivation and not feeling whole	**Core Concern** Satisfaction, stimulation and feeling good	**Core Understanding** Wholeness comes from integrating negative and positive experiences
Anxious, alternate between manic behavior and depression, joyless, cause scenes, limited self-reflection, blame others, feel easily cornered and trapped, engage in self-destructive or self-defeating behaviors	Engaging, impatient, super-fast minds generating many ideas, consider themselves quick learners, love the rush of new and stimulating experiences, unfocused, reframe negative events into positive ones	Focused, complete work effortlessly, listen well, emanate happiness and peaceful joy, spirited, deep with a true sense of wonder, inspire those around them through their calm, vital presence

LOW — MEDIUM — HIGH

8 Enneagram Type Eight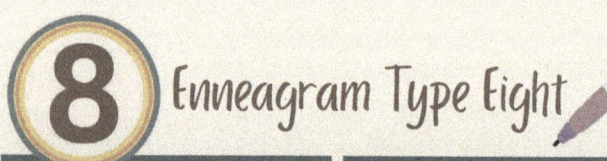

Low Self-Mastery The Bully	Medium Self-Mastery The Immovable Rock	High Self-Mastery The Truth Seeker
Core Fear Being harmed, controlled or extremely vulnerable	**Core Concern** Self-protection and showing weakness	**Core Understanding** Vulnerability is part of being human; real truth comes from integrating multiple truths
Direct to the point of cruelty, floods of anger, destructive punitive behavior, power-oriented, deteriorate into antisocial or violent behavior when they cannot contain or control their explosive anger	Sensitive and generous, controlling, dominating, aggressive, like immediate action, unmovable opinions, presence felt when quiet, need increasingly bigger challenges, angry, blaming	Manage vast energy and anger, acknowledge their vulnerability, generous, strong, open-hearted, open-minded, embrace differing opinions, grounded yet flexible, warm, deeply confident

LOW — MEDIUM — HIGH

PART 2 WHERE AM I NOW?

 Enneagram Type Nine

Low Self-Mastery The Sleeper	Medium Self-Mastery The Harmonizer	High Self-Mastery The Fully Conscious Individual
Core Fear Separation from others, being controlled and discord	**Core Concern** Stability, harmony and being heard	**Core Understanding** Unconditional regard connects everyone and everything
Pay minimal attention to themselves, low energy, ignore problems, consistently neglectful and forgetful, sluggish, immovable when pressured, become passive-aggressive, say yes but mean no, can burst forth with fury	Seek peace and harmony, mediate differences, anxious when conflict is directed at them, pursue activities that distract them, trouble asking for what they want, like routine activities, act agreeably, go along to get along	Easily take a stand, approach life actively and purposefully, voice own opinions, engaged, vital, solid, substantial, alert, serene, deeply content, "in flow", firm inner core

LOW   MEDIUM   HIGH

Notes

PART 2 WHERE AM I NOW?

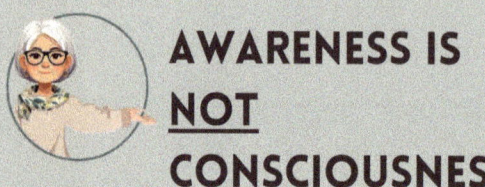

AWARENESS IS NOT CONSCIOUSNESS

Development and transformation can be thought of as forward movement on a horizontal and a vertical axis. Think of the horizontal axis as psychological development and the vertical axis as spiritual development. Growth on either axis requires accurate self-awareness, yet awareness by itself is not the same as consciousness.

Awareness	Consciousness
Specific	Broad
Attention is directed at something specific	Attention focused on larger space in which awareness occurs
Dynamic and shifting	Foundational and continuous
Helps you notice, name and track internal and external events	Incorporates all experience, perception, and thought

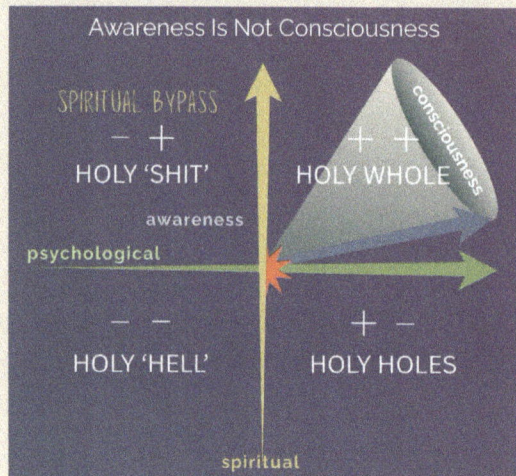

HOLY HELL

Awareness by itself is not consciousness. If you are not aware psychologically or open to spiritual awareness, you belong in the lower left quadrant: low psychologically and low spiritually.

HOLY SHIT

If you have done quite a bit of spiritual development, but not worked on your psychological growth, you belong in the upper left quadrant and are in "spiritual bypass." "Spiritual bypassing" is a psychological defense mechanism where spiritual ideas, beliefs, or practices are used to avoid or deny unresolved emotional issues and psychological needs.

HOLY HOLES

If your focus is only on psychological development, you'll make psychological progress, yet there will ultimately be holes or gaps in your psychological development and even bigger gaps or holes in your spiritual development.

HOLY WHOLE

If you are in this quadrant, it means you have been doing developmental work both spiritually and psychologically. In your journey toward wholeness, the two dimensions - psychological and spiritual - are working together to support your transformation.

PART 2 WHERE AM I NOW?

PSYCHOLOGICAL DEVELOPMENT

Psychological development and spiritual development are not the same thing. Psychological development involves horizontal movement, while spiritual development occurs on vertical axis. Psychological growth is the process by which a person's mental, emotional and behavioral responses evolve over time. The context for this includes ourselves, others and the world at large. There are three core factors involved from each Center of Intelligence for a total of 9 factors as seen here.

PSYCHOLOGICAL ASSESSMENT

DIRECTIONS

Please rate your level of psychological development based on each of the 9 factors below, three factors for each Center of Intelligence: Head, Heart and Body. Fill in the circle below each factor. To help you with your answer, you can consider the two questions below each factor.

HEAD CENTER

Awareness: the ability to recognize, in the moment, your honest thought patterns, emotional reactions and behaviors, as well as your true motivations and your impact on others

Questions:
1. Are you focusing on awareness of your patterns and not just on specific thoughts, feelings and behaviors?
2. How do you know when and if you are consciously choosing your responses, including your thoughts, versus when you are reacting out of habit?

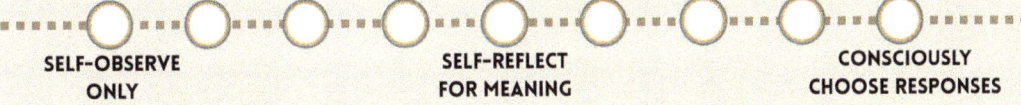

SELF-OBSERVE ONLY — SELF-REFLECT FOR MEANING — CONSCIOUSLY CHOOSE RESPONSES

PART 2 WHERE AM I NOW?

PSYCHOLOGICAL ASSESSMENT (CONTINUED)

HEAD CENTER (CONTINUED)

Accurate self-perception: has an accurate and realistic sense of self that embraces complexity and paradox, rather than maintaining and defending an idealized view of self

Questions:
1. What is your idealized self; how would you describe it?
2. How do you know if and when your type-based ego ideal is obstructing your ability to know yourself accurately?

CRAVE EGO REINFORCEMENT   OPEN TO FEEDBACK   EMBRACE MY COMPLEXITY

Objective discernment: able to discern whether your reactions are objective, rather than your imagining that something is true about someone else when it is, in fact, a projection of your hopes and fears

Questions:
1. How do you know when you are projecting; what cues do you have?
2. Do you understand the purpose projection serves for you personally?

CONSTANTLY PROJECT   SOMETIMES PROJECT   RARELY PROJECT

HEART CENTER

Motivation: accurately identify and understand your true inner drives including your inner contradictions

Questions:
1. How do you know you are probing yourself deeply, honestly and accurately?
2. Do you know the difference between expectations from others and self-motivation, between internal and external motivation?

RARELY KNOW   SOMETIMES KNOW   ACKNOWLEDGE TRUE MOTIVES

HEART CENTER (CONTINUED)

Emotional Dexterity: accurately identify own feelings and be able to process them effectively

Questions:
1. What helps you identify and process your feelings effectively and what gets in the way?
2. Do you have a bias towards any feeling groups - mad, sad, glad and afraid - and why?

HARD TO IDENTIFY FEELINGS — KNOW BUT DON'T LET GO — KNOW AND PROCESS EASILY

Responsiveness: an open, flexible and resilient response to challenges and threats, rather than a contracted or aggressive reaction

Questions:
1. How do you know when you are and are not being defensive?
2. How does your defensiveness manifest and under what circumstances?

HIGHLY DEFENSIVE — SOMETIMES DEFENSIVE — RARELY DEFENSIVE

BODY CENTER

Self-regulation: the ability to understand and effectively manage your own behavior and responses

Questions:
1. How do you know when you are being reactive; what are your cues?
2. What do you do to maximize your self-regulation and minimize your reactivity?

REACTIVE — SELF-REGULATING WITH EFFORT — REGULARLY SELF-REGULATING

PART 2 WHERE AM I NOW?

PSYCHOLOGICAL ASSESSMENT (CONTINUED)

BODY CENTER (CONTINUED)
Responsibility: being accountable for your own responses and actions, including why you do what you do and your impact on others, whether intended or not

Questions:
1. How do you know what is your responsibility, someone else's or a joint responsibility?
2. What are the subtle and blatant ways you blame others?

FEEL VICTIMIZED　　　OFTEN BLAME OTHERS　　　STRONG SENSE OF PERSONAL AGENCY

Integration: having clear access to all three Centers of Intelligence – Head, Heart, Body – so that the three Centers communicate with each other and allow you to function in an aligned, clear and productive way

Questions:
1. Do you tend to over-rely on one or two Centers of Intelligence and underuse one or more Centers?
2. Are you using each Center in its most productive ways, and do your Centers communicate and coordinate with each other?

OFTEN FEEL CONFUSED　　　SOMETIMES UNCLEAR　　　ACCESS ALL THREE CENTERS WELL

Notes

PART 2 WHERE AM I NOW?

SPIRITUAL DEVELOPMENT

Spiritual development is a vertical axis representing the process by which a person expands their mental, emotional, and somatic awareness of and relationship to something greater than the individual self. This transformation can be through the sacred, the divine, the universal, inner wisdom, deep interconnectedness, and more. There are three core factors involved from each Center of Intelligence for a total of 9 factors as seen here.

SPIRITUAL ASSESSMENT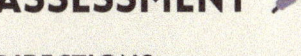

DIRECTIONS
Please rate your level of spiritual development based on each of the 9 factors below, three factors for each Center of Intelligence: Head, Heart and Body. Fill in the circle below each factor. To help you with your answer, you can consider the two questions provided.

HEAD CENTER
Humility: an attitude of deep psychological and spiritual modesty that comes from understanding our place in the larger order of things, understood best as neither arrogance nor false humility (the pretense of being modest)

Questions:
1. Can you recognize when you are acting or feeling superior to others, even subtly?
2. Can you perceive yourself accurately without exaggeration or diminishment?

PART 2 WHERE AM I NOW?

SPIRITUAL ASSESSMENT (CONTINUED)

HEAD CENTER (CONTINUED)

Truthfulness: knowing and being willing to express your authentic thoughts and feelings to yourself and others, plus having your choices and actions congruent with your principles and core values

Questions:
1. In what ways are you truthful and in what ways are you still working on being more truthful or authentic?
2. What do you think most gets in your way of being more genuine, honest, and real?

SELDOM KNOW AND/OR SHARE   SELECTIVELY TRUTHFUL   CONSISTENTLY TRUTHFUL

Non-attachment: the ability to let go of, without regret, anything you care about such as material possessions, external validation, limiting beliefs, emotions, relationships, resentments, or negativity that hinders your growth and transformation

Questions:
1. Do you know the difference between detachment and non-attachment and between caring versus holding on?
2. What makes it easier or harder for you to be non-attached (not detached)?

STRONGLY ATTACHED   SELECTIVELY ATTACHED   MINIMALLY ATTACHED

HEART CENTER

Gratitude: appreciating all aspects of life, both small and large, while cultivating a genuine thankfulness for the simplest moments and gifts

Questions:
1. When you think of your daily life, what percentage of it do you spend in gratitude?
2. What gets in your way of feeling more grateful?

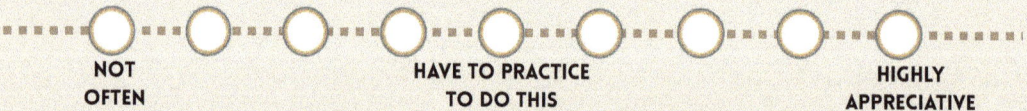

NOT OFTEN   HAVE TO PRACTICE TO DO THIS   HIGHLY APPRECIATIVE

PART 2 WHERE AM I NOW?

HEART CENTER (CONTINUED)

Compassion: genuinely and deeply caring about the well-being of others in a balanced way, while understanding their struggles with a compassion and empathy that extends way beyond your immediate circle

Questions:
1. How compassionate do you think you are?
2. What obstacles do you face in being fully compassionate?

RARELY CARE　　　SOMETIMES CARE　　　DEEPLY CARE

Acceptance: a deep sense of self-acceptance, including strengths and weaknesses, without judgment, as well as a non-judgmental attitude towards others, including those who are not like you

Questions:
1. Are you more accepting of yourself or of others and why?
2. What parts of yourself are the hardest to accept?

HIGHLY JUDGMENTAL　　　SOMETIMES JUDGMENTAL　　　ACCEPTING OF SELF AND OTHERS

BODY CENTER

Service: a desire to contribute positively to the well-being of other people and the world, as manifested by engaging in acts of kindness, service, and actions that make a difference

Questions:

1. How often do you currently engage in true acts of service and what has been your pattern with this over time?

2. When you have done something of service, what is it you expect in return (from yourself or others)?

SELDOM ENGAGE　　　SOMETIMES ENGAGE　　　REGULARLY ENGAGE

PART 2 WHERE AM I NOW?

SPIRITUAL ASSESSMENT (CONTINUED)

BODY CENTER (CONTINUED)

Receptivity: the ability to be open, responsive and engaged with new people, ideas and experiences

Questions:
1. In the past, have you been close-minded, open-minded or in between?
2. When you are more receptive and open, what do you experience somatically, emotionally and mentally?

CLOSE-MINDED — OPENNESS VARIES — OPEN-MINDED

Presence: the ability to be in the present moment, while being fully aware of your own internal reactions and what is occurring in your immediate environment, rather than being preoccupied with the past or the future

Questions:
1. What does it mean to "be in presence"?
2. How do you know if you are "being in presence" or faking it?

RARELY — SOMETIMES — EASY TO DO

Notes

PART 2 WHERE AM I NOW?

TRUE SELF – FALSE SELF

Ours is a journey from our false self – our ego or lower self – to our true self, higher self or essence. What do these concepts really mean in terms of how we think, feel, and behave? The information below provides some insights.

	True Self (higher self)	False Self (lower self)
Definition	Who you really are	Who you want to appear to be
Experienced as	Open, connected, peaceful, creative, expansive, allowing	Contracted, performative, anxious, restless, controlling
Roots or origins	Being, presence	Doing, socialization
Thoughts	Quiet, inner knowing, nonjudgmental	Critical, agitated, vengeful, prescriptive
Feelings	"I am enough as I am."	"I am not...;" "I am not OK!"
Behavior	Receptive, gracious	Automatic, habitual, reactive, protective
Motivation	Love, truth, freedom, connectedness	Fear, shame, anger, comparison
Impact on others	Invites authenticity, openness, puts others at ease	Causes confusion, guardedness, emotional distance
Spiritual impact	Sacred, humble, beyond ego	Striving, deceitful, egoistic
Related concepts	Essence, soul, presence, being, higher self	Ego, personality, type, persona, lower self

PART 2 WHERE AM I NOW?

TRUE SELF – FALSE SELF (CONTINUED)

Our False Self, our Enneagram type, contains our habits of mind, emotions and behaviors, as well as our deepest motivational structure and our type-based worldview. Within our type-based habits are two energetic forces, one that moves forward to pursue our desires – the affirming 1st force – and an opposite energetic force, the denying or 2nd force. The 1st force is one of energetic expansion, while the 2nd force is that of contraction and resistance.

Once we name, experience and hold these two oppositional forces simultaneously, the 3rd force emerges. This freeing force reconciles the first two forces in a brand new and creative way that neither desires nor resists. From this dynamic, our True Self emerges.

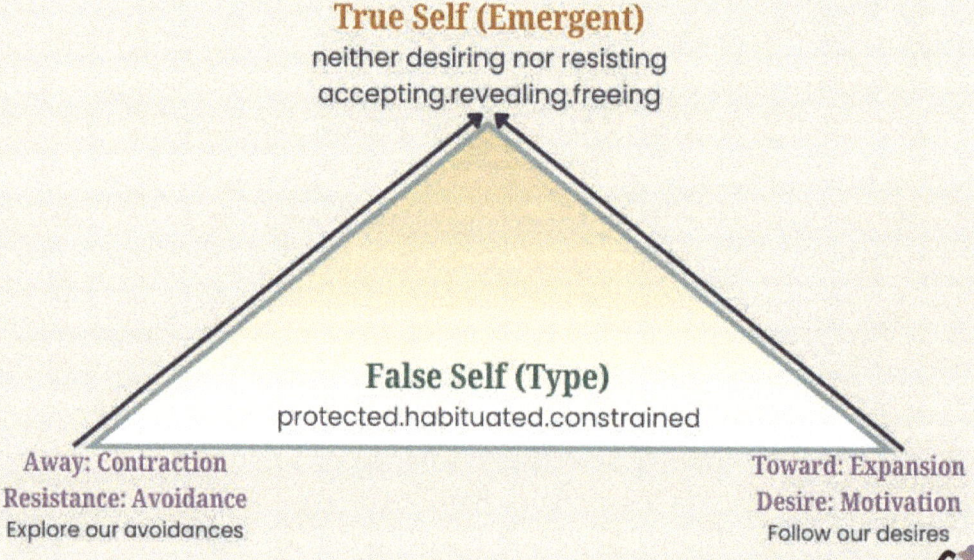

When do I feel most like myself – without effort, without roles? This is closer to my True Self.

What patterns or personas do I use when I feel unsafe, unseen, or unworthy? This is closer to my False Self.

How do I know when I am reacting from habit (False Self) versus responding from presence (True Self)?

PART 2 WHERE AM I NOW?

TRUE SELF–FALSE SELF BY ENNEAGRAM TYPE

Enneagram Type One

TRUE SELF (ESSENCE)
Serenity, inherent goodness, inner balance

FALSE SELF (TYPE STRUCTURE)
Compulsive perfection, rigid self-control, self-judgment

REFLECTION QUESTION
"What if goodness arises through presence, not perfection?"

TRUE SELF QUESTIONS

Can I allow imperfection without needing to correct it? ☐ yes ☐ no ☐ sometimes

Am I grounded in inner calm versus immersed in inner criticism? ☐ yes ☐ no ☐ sometimes

Are my actions guided by wisdom, not just by what's "right"? ☐ yes ☐ no ☐ sometimes

FALSE SELF (TYPE) QUESTIONS

Do I become tense when something is wrong or out of order? ☐ yes ☐ no ☐ sometimes

Am I regularly irritated by flaws – my own and those of others? ☐ yes ☐ no ☐ sometimes

Am I constantly judging and intolerant of mistakes? ☐ yes ☐ no ☐ sometimes

PART 2 WHERE AM I NOW?

TRUE SELF–FALSE SELF BY ENNEAGRAM TYPE

Enneagram Type Two

TRUE SELF (ESSENCE)
Unconditional love, generosity of spirit, open-hearted presence

FALSE SELF (TYPE STRUCTURE)
Needing to feel worthy by being needed, people-pleasing, self-neglect

REFLECTION QUESTION
"What if I am loved without needing to earn it by giving to others?"

TRUE SELF QUESTIONS

Do I give from pure generosity, not a need to be needed? ☐ yes ☐ no ☐ sometimes

Am I connected to myself as much as I feel connected to others? ☐ yes ☐ no ☐ sometimes

Can I receive care as freely as I give it? ☐ yes ☐ no ☐ sometimes

FALSE SELF (TYPE) QUESTIONS

Am I anticipating others' needs as a way to earn love? ☐ yes ☐ no ☐ sometimes

Do I feel invisible unless I'm being helpful? ☐ yes ☐ no ☐ sometimes

Can I even imagine not trying to support others all the time? ☐ yes ☐ no ☐ sometimes

PART 2 WHERE AM I NOW?

TRUE SELF–FALSE SELF BY ENNEAGRAM TYPE

Enneagram Type Three

TRUE SELF (ESSENCE)
Radiance, intrinsic worth, authentic presence

FALSE SELF (TYPE STRUCTURE)
Image-driven success, constantly proving their value, utilitarian use of self and others

REFLECTION QUESTION
"What if I stop performing and can still be seen and valued?"

TRUE SELF QUESTIONS

Am I engaging life from a place of authenticity and not image?   ☐ yes ☐ no ☐ sometimes

Do I believe that I am of value aside from my accomplishments?   ☐ yes ☐ no ☐ sometimes

Can I rest or "be" in a simple state of being?   ☐ yes ☐ no ☐ sometimes

FALSE SELF (TYPE) QUESTIONS

Am I managing how I appear (my persona) instead of being real?   ☐ yes ☐ no ☐ sometimes

Am I constantly chasing goals and creating plans?   ☐ yes ☐ no ☐ sometimes

Do I feel lost without knowing my roles and related expectations?   ☐ yes ☐ no ☐ sometimes

PART 2 WHERE AM I NOW?

TRUE SELF–FALSE SELF BY ENNEAGRAM TYPE

Enneagram Type Four

TRUE SELF (ESSENCE)
Depth, beauty, profound presence

FALSE SELF (TYPE STRUCTURE)
Longing, emotional intensity, preoccupation with "Who am I?"

REFLECTION QUESTION
"What if I can I accept what is and not be preoccupied with what's missing?"

TRUE SELF QUESTIONS

Am I grounded in what is real and beautiful right now? ☐ yes ☐ no ☐ sometimes

Do I feel whole without needing to amplify my intensity? ☐ yes ☐ no ☐ sometimes

Can I enjoy how I am like others, not how I am different? ☐ yes ☐ no ☐ sometimes

FALSE SELF (TYPE) QUESTIONS

Am I romanticizing suffering or longing for what's missing? ☐ yes ☐ no ☐ sometimes

Do I mistake feelings that are familiar for feelings that are deep? ☐ yes ☐ no ☐ sometimes

Do I have difficulty accepting myself as enough just as I am? ☐ yes ☐ no ☐ sometimes

PART 2 WHERE AM I NOW?

TRUE SELF–FALSE SELF BY ENNEAGRAM TYPE

Enneagram Type Five

5

TRUE SELF (ESSENCE)
Clarity, spaciousness, penetrating insight

FALSE SELF (TYPE STRUCTURE)
Withholding, detachment, mental and emotional hoarding

REFLECTION QUESTION
"What if I can open up and be fully in the world without feeling drained?"

TRUE SELF QUESTIONS

Am I spacious, not contracted, and connected to the world?	☐ yes ☐ no ☐ sometimes
Can I trust I don't need to rely solely on my own resources?	☐ yes ☐ no ☐ sometimes
Do I feel safe and take pleasure in showing up fully?	☐ yes ☐ no ☐ sometimes

FALSE SELF (TYPE) QUESTIONS

Am I retreating into my mind to avoid engagement?	☐ yes ☐ no ☐ sometimes
Do I disconnect from feelings in real time without recognizing it?	☐ yes ☐ no ☐ sometimes
Am I using thought to replace experience?	☐ yes ☐ no ☐ sometimes

PART 2 WHERE AM I NOW?

TRUE SELF–FALSE SELF BY ENNEAGRAM TYPE

Enneagram Type Six — **6**

TRUE SELF (ESSENCE)
Courage, grounded faith, inner knowing

FALSE SELF (TYPE STRUCTURE)
Anxiety, doubt, over-questioning

REFLECTION QUESTION
"What if I trusted what I know without a need to rely on others' authority?"

TRUE SELF QUESTIONS

Am I grounded in trust, both in myself and the unfolding of life? ☐ yes ☐ no ☐ sometimes

Can I act from my inner authority without external reassurance? ☐ yes ☐ no ☐ sometimes

Do I feel courageous and safe even in the face of uncertainty? ☐ yes ☐ no ☐ sometimes

FALSE SELF (TYPE) QUESTIONS

Am I recycling doubt and second-guessing myself? ☐ yes ☐ no ☐ sometimes

Am I over-listening to the loud voice of my fear? ☐ yes ☐ no ☐ sometimes

Am I trying to outsource my inner security? ☐ yes ☐ no ☐ sometimes

PART 2 WHERE AM I NOW?

TRUE SELF–FALSE SELF BY ENNEAGRAM TYPE

Enneagram Type Seven

TRUE SELF (ESSENCE)
True joy, freedom based on conscious choice, endless possibility

FALSE SELF (TYPE STRUCTURE)
Avoidance of pain and discomfort, constant need for stimulation, no limits

REFLECTION QUESTION
"What richness might I find if I stay with what's here right now?"

TRUE SELF QUESTIONS

Can I savor the moment for extended periods of time? ☐ yes ☐ no ☐ sometimes

Am I willing to stay with discomfort without needing to escape? ☐ yes ☐ no ☐ sometimes

Does joy arise naturally in me instead of my chasing stimulation? ☐ yes ☐ no ☐ sometimes

FALSE SELF (TYPE) QUESTIONS

Am I avoiding feelings and experiences by moving on so quickly? ☐ yes ☐ no ☐ sometimes

Is my excitement actually covering my fear or pain? ☐ yes ☐ no ☐ sometimes

Do I avoid what's unfinished in me that I don't want to feel? ☐ yes ☐ no ☐ sometimes

PART 2 WHERE AM I NOW?

TRUE SELF–FALSE SELF BY ENNEAGRAM TYPE

Enneagram Type Eight

TRUE SELF (ESSENCE)
Vitality, openness, life force in the service of truth

FALSE SELF (TYPE STRUCTURE)
Control, intensity, psychological and physical armor

REFLECTION QUESTION
"What if softness and receptivity are more powerful than strength and force?"

TRUE SELF QUESTIONS

Am I using my strength in the service of love or control? ☐ yes ☐ no ☐ sometimes

Am I allowing vulnerability to coexist with power? ☐ yes ☐ no ☐ sometimes

Can I be soft and innocent without feeling weak? ☐ yes ☐ no ☐ sometimes

FALSE SELF (TYPE) QUESTIONS

Am I often in fight mode but don't know what I'm really fighting? ☐ yes ☐ no ☐ sometimes

Do I realize how physically and emotionally armored I am? ☐ yes ☐ no ☐ sometimes

Do I know who or what I am protecting and why? ☐ yes ☐ no ☐ sometimes

PART 2 WHERE AM I NOW?

TRUE SELF–FALSE SELF BY ENNEAGRAM TYPE

Enneagram Type Nine

TRUE SELF (ESSENCE)
Unity, presence, undivided being

FALSE SELF (TYPE STRUCTURE)
Numbing, merging, forgetting self

REFLECTION QUESTION
"What if I found my voice, embraced my energy, and claimed my space?"

TRUE SELF QUESTIONS

Am I fully embodied and available to myself and others? ☐ yes ☐ no ☐ sometimes

Do I know what I want, and can I express my desires to others? ☐ yes ☐ no ☐ sometimes

Can I feel whole without merging with something outside myself? ☐ yes ☐ no ☐ sometimes

FALSE SELF (TYPE) QUESTIONS

Do I go along with others in order to avoid conflict? ☐ yes ☐ no ☐ sometimes

Do I numb myself to important things, including myself? ☐ yes ☐ no ☐ sometimes

Do I often defer in situations that need my full presence? ☐ yes ☐ no ☐ sometimes

PART 2 WHERE AM I NOW?

LAW OF THREE

In any process of creation or **change**, these three forces are always at play; without all three, no real transformation can occur. Change may happen, but not transformation.

AFFIRMING FORCE
1st force — initiating energy (desire, action, growth, movement)

DENYING FORCE
2nd force — opposing energy (resistance, anchoring, inertia, fear)

RECONCILING FORCE
3rd force — harmonizing energy (transforms tension from first two forces into something new)

RECONCILING
THIRD FORCE
INTEGRATES AND TRANSFORMS

PUSHES BACK

INITIATES CHANGE

DENYING
SECOND FORCE

AFFIRMING
FIRST FORCE

As you think about yourself, do you live more in the affirming or the denying force? Does this relate to your Enneagram type or perhaps something else in your background?

PART 2 WHERE AM I NOW?

REFLECTION

Reflect on your self-assessments and where you think you are on your development and transformation journey. Reflect on your lifelong journey from False Self to True Self. Where are you on your path? What excites you as you move forward? What do you want to pay special attention to?

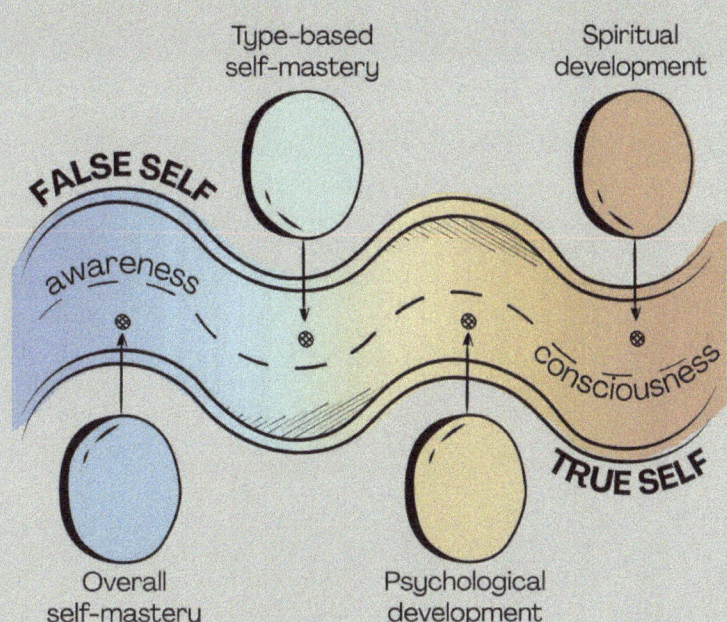

PART 2 WHERE AM I NOW?

PART 2 HIGHLIGHTS

REMEMBER
Be realistic about where to start your development

Understand the three forces underlying your growth: affirming, denying, reconciling

Embrace the emergent

DO'S
Be honest with yourself
Be self-reflective
Be curious

DONT'S
Judge yourself
Stop at your first answer
Look outward for what is inward

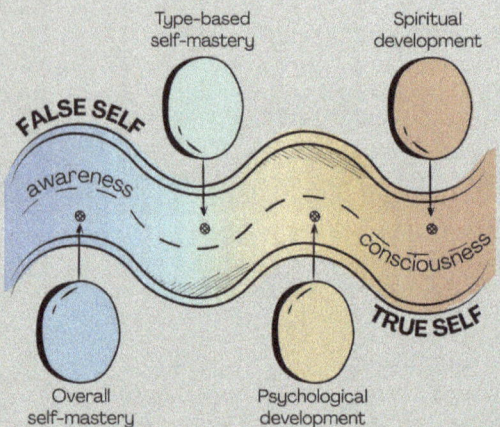

REFLECTIONS

"The curious paradox is that when I accept myself just as I am, then I can change."
- Carl Rogers

"When I let go of who I am, I become what I might be."
- Lao Tzu

WHAT AM I MOVING TOWARD?

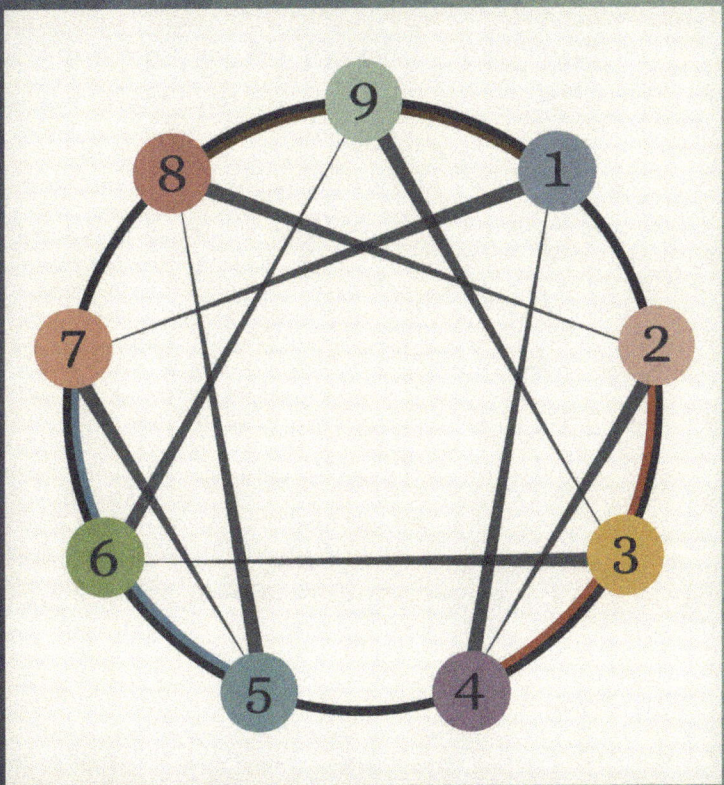

PART THREE

PART 3: WHAT AM I MOVING TOWARD?

TABLE OF CONTENTS

Introduction	63
Law of Three Revisited	64
Somatic Power	65
The Importance of Imagination	66
Development Pathways	67
Enneagram as a Map	70
Awareness, Exploration and Practice	81
Awareness	82
Exploration	88
Practice	92
Highlights	94

INTRODUCTION

Have you wondered why there is such a gravitational attraction to working with positive energy as we engage in development work? Think about the abundance of affirmations, the emphasis on giving positive feedback, managing based on a person's strengths, and the current focus on the importance of gratitude.

Positive energy that affirms feels good. It creates feelings of happiness, optimism, reduces stress, and improves motivation. When we feel positive, our brains release dopamine, serotonin, endorphins, and oxytocin, which are collectively known as the "happy hormones." Positivity even boosts our immune system.

Now that you have a better sense of where you are in your development journey, Part 3 emphasizes the 1st force of the Law of Three – the affirming force – by providing activities that focus on the power of the positive, with exercises to increase your somatic power. You can explore the Enneagram Development Map showing the multiple paths for development, rather than just one way for each type.

Have you ever used the Enneagram as a map, not just on a wall but on the floor? As a floor map, the Enneagram symbol helps us fully embody the insights and wisdom of the symbol itself. You'll get step-by-step instructions on how to do this using six different processes.

Profound as all the above is, there are even more great activities related to awareness, exploration, and practice. Enjoy!

PART 3 WHAT AM I MOVING TOWARD?

LAW OF THREE REVISITED

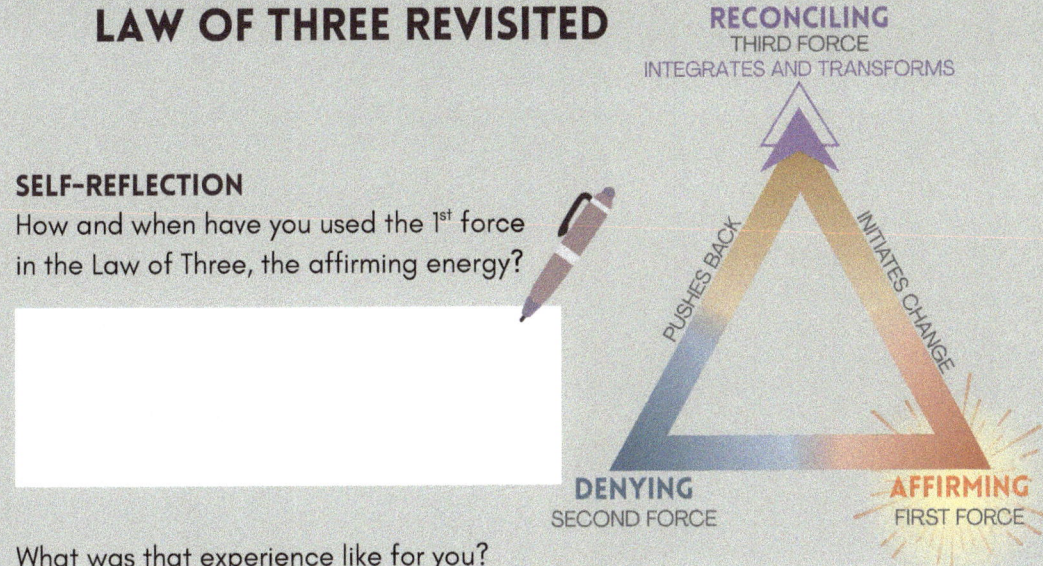

SELF-REFLECTION
How and when have you used the 1st force in the Law of Three, the affirming energy?

What was that experience like for you?

POWER OF POSITIVITY

Positive thinking is important in self-development because it shifts our inner orientation toward possibility, resilience, and growth.

Activates the growth mindset
- Encourages learning from mistakes instead of being derailed by them
- Supports the belief that change and development are possible

Builds psychological resilience
- Helps you bounce back from setbacks with greater ease
- Fosters emotional agility by reducing the impact of fear or failure

Increases motivation and engagement
- Positivity fuels action; negativity often leads to paralysis or avoidance
- Creates momentum toward goals and encourages follow-through

Rewires the brain toward well-being
- Practicing positive thinking strengthens neural pathways associated with optimism, calm, and confidence
- Over time, positivity becomes a default rather than a forced mindset

PART 3 WHAT AM I MOVING TOWARD?

SOMATIC POWER

Personal power has mental and emotional components, but the actual experience is primarily somatic or body-based. Once you find your somatic personal power center - through one of three ways - you create a power bubble all around you and then keep expanding your bubble. Credit for this goes to Wendy Palmer from her book, *Leadership Embodiment*.

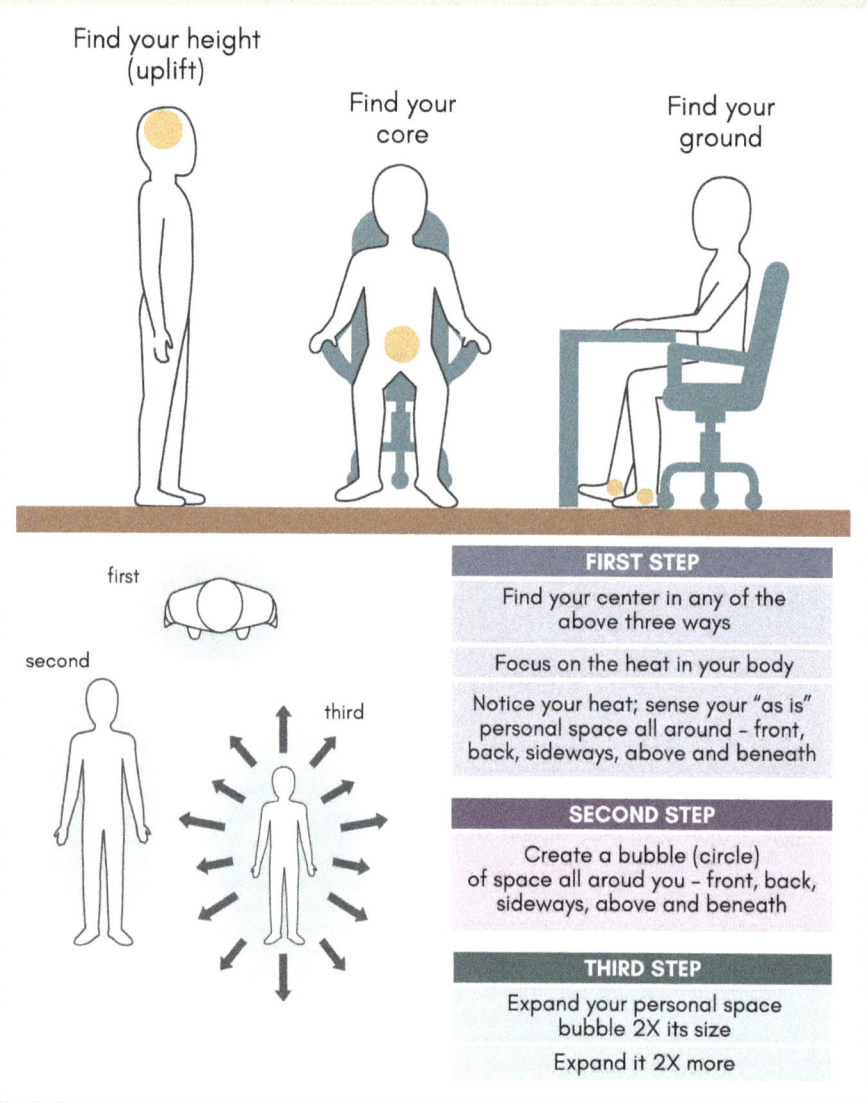

Find your center in each of these three ways: standing up and centering in your head; sitting down and centering in your belly; sitting down and centering in both ankles. Each time you find your center, create an energetic bubble around you in all directions. Then expand the energy in your center gradually in all directions. What do you experience now? Try each place of centering to experience what works best for you.

PART 3 WHAT AM I MOVING TOWARD?

THE IMPORTANCE OF IMAGINATION

Take a moment to reflect and imagine. Imagination is essential for visioning, and if we can't envision ourselves doing or being something, it becomes harder to attain.

Breathe in a relaxed and rhythmic way. Inhale through your nose and when you exhale, do so through your mouth. This allows the air to fill and relax you more. Imagine a horizon, a beautiful horizon where something is slowly emerging. Experience and observe that which is emerging, revealing itself to you. It's something you desire, you want, you aspire to. What is it? How do you experience it? Does it give you a message or is there something you'd like to ask it? Feel free to engage as you wish.

PART 3 WHAT AM I MOVING TOWARD?

DEVELOPMENT PATHWAYS

Have you ever thought or been told that there is only one best path for development and transformation using the Enneagram? If so, please think again! There are multiple different paths that can be used separately, sequentially or simultaneously.

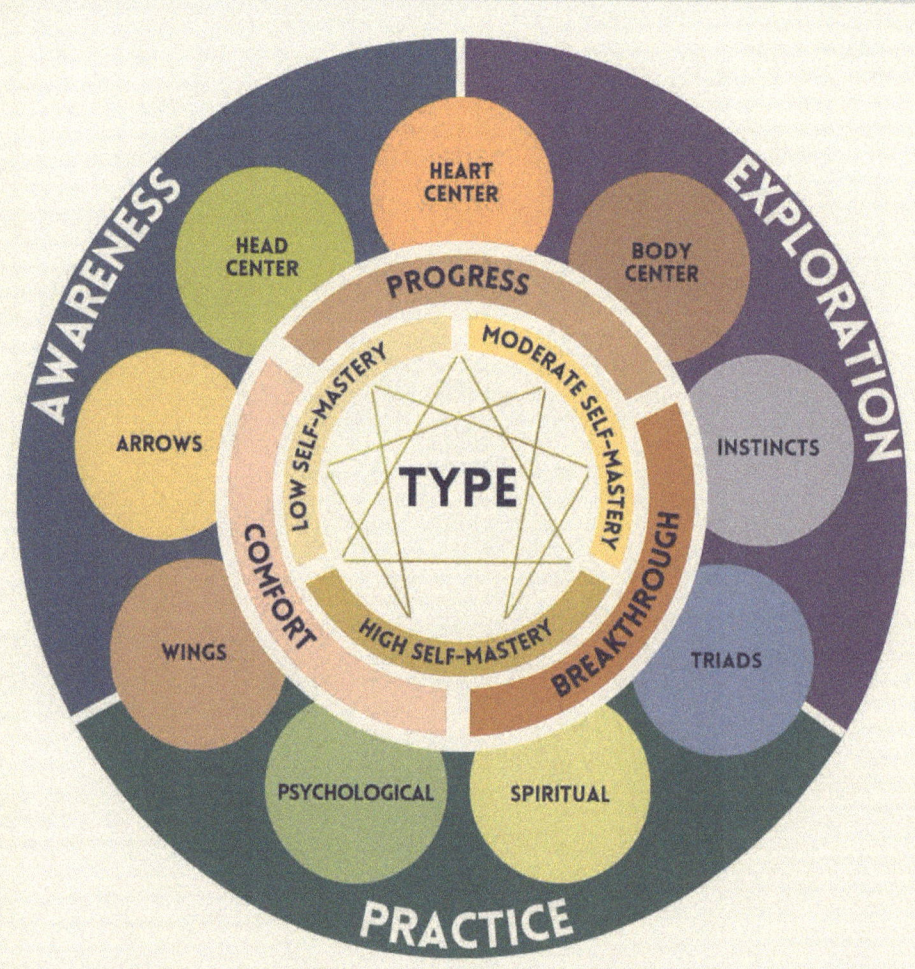

Head Center Path
- Focus: Thinking patterns (fixation), mental chatter, beliefs, self-negations
- Path includes: Mindfulness, assumption challenges, inquiry, mental clarity

Heart Center Path
- Focus: Emotional patterns (passion/vice), emotional range, emotional depth, emotional triggers, reactivity
- Path includes: Vulnerability work, empathy development, emotional regulation

PART 3 WHAT AM I MOVING TOWARD?

Body Center Path
- Focus: Somatic awareness and access, grounding, embodiment
- Path includes: Breathwork, movement, body work, somatic release

Centers Integration Path
- Focus: Understanding type-based use and misuse of each Center, identifying Centers' misalignments, embracing paradox
- Path includes: Head, Heart and Body Center work, productive access to each Center, communication and synergy between and among Centers

Instincts Path
- Focus: Instincts, instinctual needs, distortions, subtype creation
- Path includes: Awareness of and development based on subtype triggers, relaxing type-based passion to free our instincts, balancing instinctual needs

Triads Path
- Focus: Growth and transformation through approaches that utilize the multiple triangles within the Enneagram model
- Paths include: 3 Centers of Intelligence (Head, Heart, Body); Optimistic-Competency-Intensity triads (2-7-9, 1-3-5, 4-6-8); Invisible Triangles (3-6-9 attachment); (1-4-7 frustration); (2-5-8 rejection)

Spiritual Path
- Focus: Essence, surrender, acceptance, non-dual perspectives
- Path includes: Meditations, presence, contemplation, humility

Psychological Path
- Focus: Mental, emotional and behavioral patterns, defense mechanisms, ego ideals
- Path includes: Practices to address healthier mental, emotional and behavioral patterns, relaxing defensive strategies, become more self-regulating

Wings Path
- Focus: Accessing wings and wing usage
- Path includes: Enhancing use and flexibility of wing qualities for use as resources and growth paths

Arrows Path
- Focus: Understanding dynamic qualities and energies of the arrows
- Path includes: Consciously integrating arrow lines as resources on path to wholeness

PART 3 WHAT AM I MOVING TOWARD?

SELF-MASTERY LEVEL

You also need to consider your current self-mastery level and the level to which you aspire. You can't jump from low to high self-mastery; it's a more developmental process than that. Also, you don't want to select a path for lower self-mastery if you are actually at a much higher level right now. These hints might be helpful.

Low Self-Mastery: slow down to reflect on your responses and choices, seek support systems, cultivate your awareness

Moderate Self-Mastery: maintain your momentum, move beyond your comfort zone (take some risks), embrace self-regulation

High Self-Mastery: experiment with new perspectives, pursue wholeness and emergence, embrace paradox and complexity

CHANGE DESIRED

Also consider the degree of change you are currently seeking. Comfort? Progress? Breakthrough?

Comfort: Use generic activities or type-based targeted practices that give short-term, focused relief and are based on specific short-term needs and goals.

Progress: Focus on core type-based issues using all three Centers of Intelligence, plus arrows, wings, Centers and subtypes.

Breakthrough: Engage both the psychological and spiritual paths, plus the three Centers of Intelligence, instinct-based development and the various Enneagram triangles using the Law of Three.

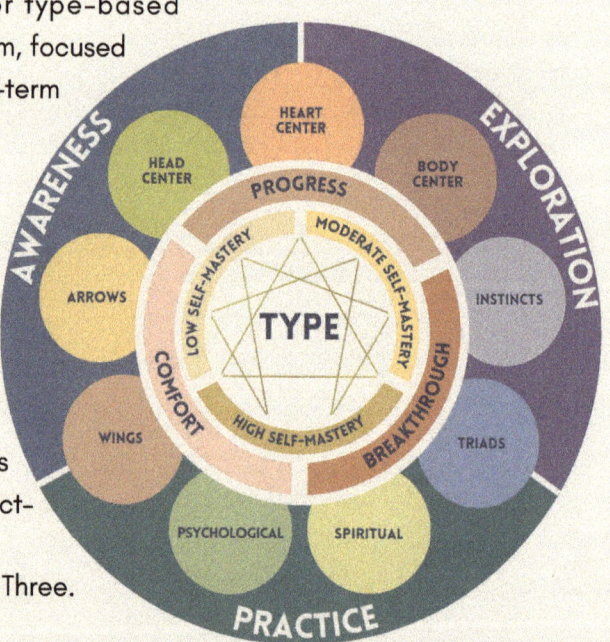

PART 3 WHAT AM I MOVING TOWARD?

ENNEAGRAM AS A MAP

NINE TYPE COLORS
Distinct colors reflecting the energetic quality of each type

The Enneagram is far more than a description of nine different Enneagram types. It is also a map of process and growth. In the map we're using, the colors have been carefully chosen, so you might be interested in their meaning.

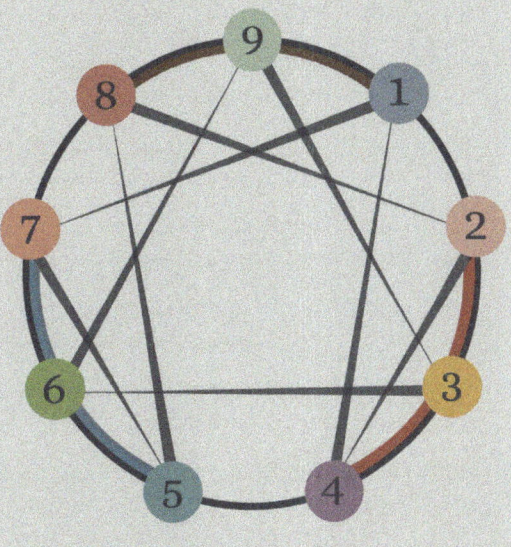

Type	Color	Meaning
1	Slate Blue	Integrity, clarity
2	Soft Rose	Warmth, care
3	Golden Ochre	Drive, achievement
4	Deep Plum	Depth, identity
5	Steel Teal	Detachment, perception
6	Olive Green	Caution, loyalty
7	Coral Orange	Joy, spontaneity
8	Brick Red	Power, presence
9	Sage/Mist	Harmony, flow

CENTERS OF INTELLIGENCE COLORS

Head Center
Core qualities Mental strategies, security, ideas, planning
Color Smokey blue reflecting introspection, analysis, and the airy or detached quality of mental activity

Heart Center
Core qualities Image, emotion, connection, identity
Color Warm red conveying warmth, emotional vibrancy, and a strong desire for recognition and connection

Body Center
Core qualities Gut instinct, control, boundaries, autonomy, presence
Color Earthy brown symbolizing grounding, power, and somatic embodiment

PART 3 WHAT AM I MOVING TOWARD?

 ENNEAGRAM AS A MAP

Here are specific guidelines and processes for using the Enneagram as a map. These guidelines are for use with yourself or with others. When fully engaged, the person on the map accesses deep insights and resources from all three Centers of Intelligence: Head, Heart and Body.

GUIDING SOMEONE ON THE MAP

Stay neutral and objective

Don't step on the map yourself

If you have thoughts, you can share them at the end of the map work

Have a process in mind, yet follow the person's emergent path

Avoid interpretation

Ask, periodically, what the person is experiencing

Make sure the person on the map is embodied while doing the map work

Pay attention to changes and ask about them

    Voice tone, volume, speech

    Body posture

    Facial expressions

    Other non-verbal cues

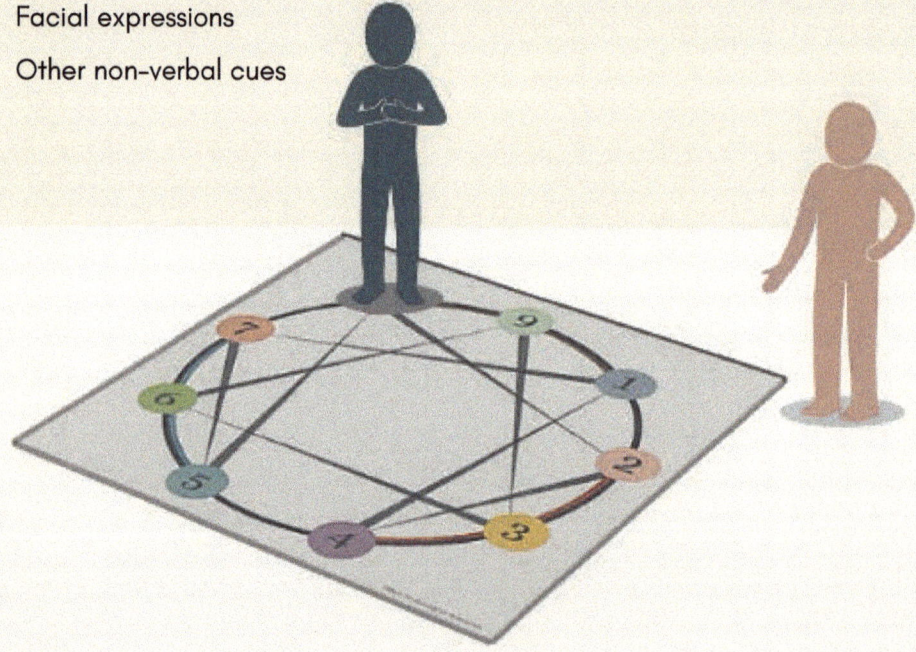

PART 3 WHAT AM I MOVING TOWARD?

WHAT QUESTIONS TO ASK THE MAP

The map likes sincere, honest, open-ended yet specific questions

Don't ask questions where the answer is already known

Yes/No questions don't invite a response from the map

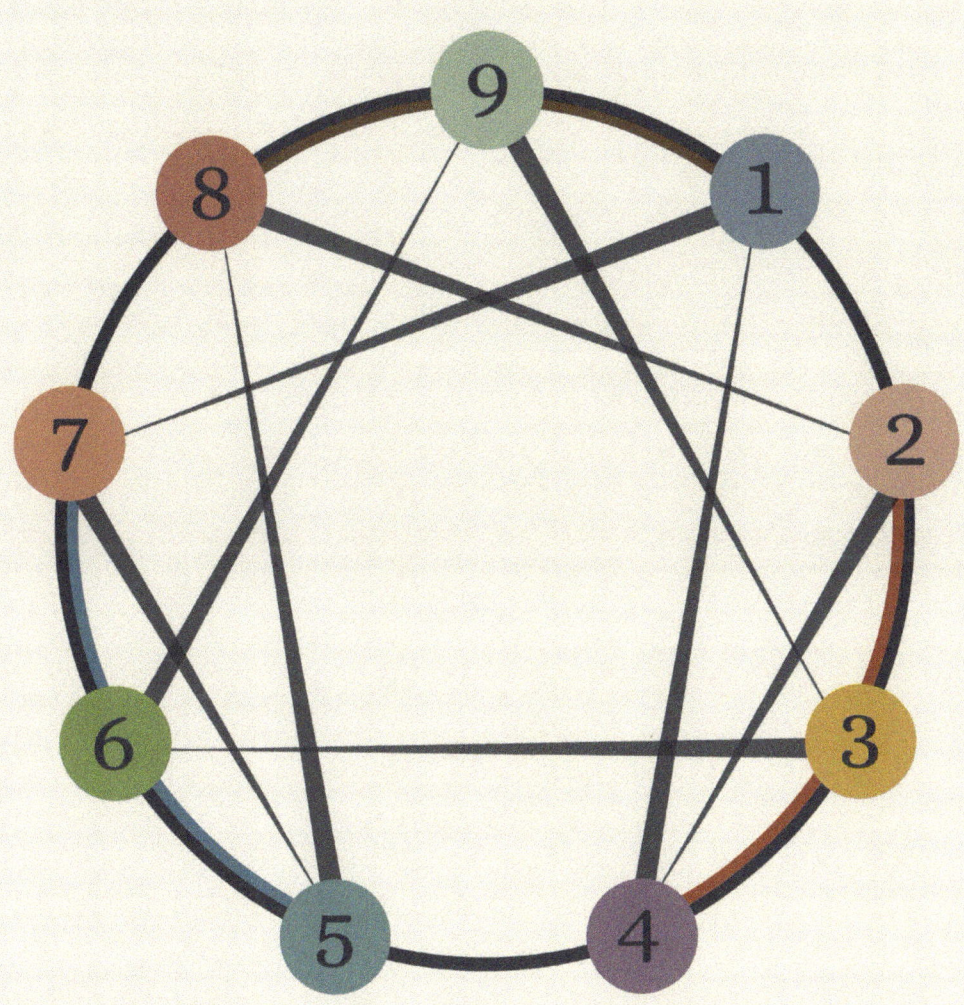

PART 3 WHAT AM I MOVING TOWARD?

INSTRUCTIONS: HOW TO USE THE MAP
SELF-REFLECTION

These instructions offer step-by-step processes you can use in your Enneagram map work. You can use them for your own exploration and development work, during sessions with clients for their development, or in your training programs to help clients solve a variety of different challenges. You can read the instructions aloud or paraphrase them as you go. Either way, the clarity and flow matter more than sticking to the exact wording.

Before you begin on the map, in most cases, the person on the map usually stands on their own Enneagram type number. Have them pause, feel into the energy of that type, and ask their question aloud (or silently if preferred). Let the response arise from the body, not the head, and invite them to say it aloud. Once they are grounded, guide them through the steps below.

PROCESS #1: WINGS AND ARROWS
A 10-Step Process for Insight, Clarity, and Growth

Use this with individuals or groups to explore...
Decision-making
Problem-solving
Development planning
Gaining fresh perspectives

Step 1: Begin at your type
Ask your question. Let the answer rise up through you and speak it aloud.

Step 2: Move to your more familiar wing
Walk slowly along the circle. Ask the same question and say aloud the insights and feelings you have from this type number.

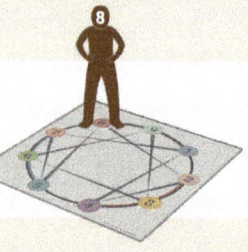

TIP:
Wings are the two numbers directly next to your type on the circle. Most people relate more to one wing than the other.

PART 3 WHAT AM I MOVING TOWARD?

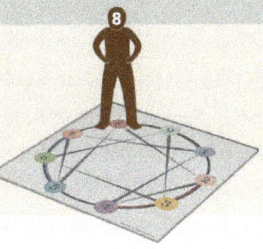

Step 3: Return to your type
Walk back slowly. No talking. Just breathe. Let it settle.

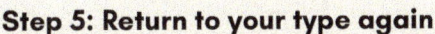

Step 4: Now go to your other wing
Walk slowly along the circle. Ask the question again. Say what emerges.

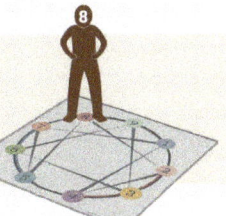

Step 5: Return to your type again
Walk back, breathe quietly. Let things integrate.

Step 6: Move to your more familiar arrow
Walk slowly to one of your two connected arrow types (one points toward you, one points away). Ask the same question. Let your response emerge and speak it.

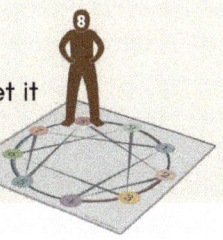

Step 7: Back to your type
Return slowly. Stand, breathe, don't speak. Let it integrate inside you.

Step 8: Explore your other arrow
Walk to your second arrow type. Ask your question again. Say aloud the insights and feelings you have from this type number.

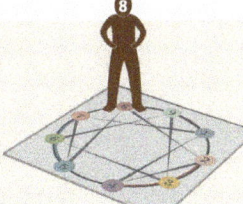

Step 9: Back to your type one last time
Back you go, slowly. Stand in silence. Let the insights from all types start to integrate.

Step 10: Reflect and share
Ask: *What are you noticing now? What answer feels most true? Which type's response had the biggest impact on you?*

Let them speak freely and fully.

> **TIP**
> Encourage the person on the map not to rush or overthink. Let each step be embodied. The answers that arise from the body's wisdom often hold more truth than what comes from mental analysis alone.

PART 3 WHAT AM I MOVING TOWARD?

PROCESS #2: AROUND THE CIRCLE

A 10-Step Process for Insight, Clarity, and Growth
Use this process when you want to help someone...
Explore many different perspectives
Clarify or question their Enneagram type
Track something that's evolving over time

Step 1: Stand on the map
Begin at Type 9, unless there's a strong reason to start somewhere else. Ask your question and say the answer aloud.

Step 2: Move to the next type
Walk to the next number in clockwise order (Type 9 → 1 → 2, etc.). Feel the energy of that number. Ask the same question. Speak your answer out loud.

TIP
Always move clockwise. The Enneagram is actually a 3D spiral; clockwise movement represents forward motion, new possibilities, and growth. Counter-clockwise movement pulls us toward the past.

Steps 3–9: Continue around the circle
Keep going around the circle, moving one type at a time in order. At each type number, pause, experience that type somatically, ask the question, say the answer out loud.

TIP
Your question may shift as you move. That's normal. If a new version of the question feels more true, use that instead.

Step 10: Return to the type where you started
Stand on that type. Feel the energy again. Ask: *What did I learn from this journey? What answers or insights are emerging now?* Speak aloud whatever wants to be said.

PART 3 WHAT AM I MOVING TOWARD?

PROCESS #3: CENTRAL TRIANGLE: 9 (AWAKE), 3 (HONEST), 6 (COURAGEOUS)

A 4-Step Process for Insight, Clarity, and Growth

Use this process when someone wants to explore...
Important issues they've been avoiding
Psychological shadows
Clarity around purpose and action

Step 1: Start at Type 9
Stand at Type 9. Take a moment there – feel the energy under your feet. Ask yourself: *What do I need to be awake to?* Let the answer rise and speak it aloud. Keep answering as long as responses continue to come.

TIP
Encourage specificity in the question. General questions get general answers. Invite the participant to go deep.

Step 2: Move to Type 3
Walk the arrow line from 9 to 3. Walk slowly with intention and feel the shift in energy. Once you arrive at Type 3, ask: *What do I need to be really honest about – especially in terms of what I just became awake to?* Let the answer emerge and speak it aloud.

Step 3: Move to Type 6
Now walk the arrow line from 3 to 6. Again, slow steps. Let the energy guide you. Once you're standing at 6, ask: *What do I need to be courageous about – especially when it comes to acting on what I experienced and learned at 9 and 3?* Speak your answer as it arises.

Step 4: Return to Type 9
Walk the arrow line from 6 back to 9. Once you are there, take a deep breath, and ask yourself: *So what is the answer to my original question?* Let everything integrate. Say the final answer aloud.

PART 3 WHAT AM I MOVING TOWARD?

PROCESS #4: HEXAD DIRECTION 1 (AGAINST THE ARROWS)
1 → 7 → 5 → 8 → 2 → 4 → 1

A 7-Step Process for Awareness, Introspection, and Growth

Use this process when participants want to explore...
Extra insight on a situation
Unspoken or unresolved elements
Areas of curiosity and intuition

Step 1: Start at Type 1
Stand at Type 1. Ground yourself. Feel your feet on the map and the energy of Type 1. Ask your question out loud. Speak the answer as it arises.

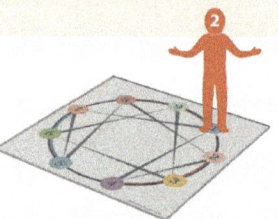

Step 2: Move to Type 7
Walk along the arrow line to Type 7. Take your time. Once you arrive, ask the same question again. Speak the answer out loud.

TIP
Always walk on the actual arrow lines slowly and mindfully. Pay attention to how the energy changes between types. It matters.

Step 3: Move to Type 5
Walk slowly along the arrow line from Type 7 to Type 5. Stand still. Ask your question and speak whatever insights or feelings arise.

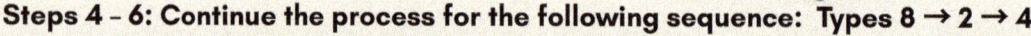

Steps 4 – 6: Continue the process for the following sequence: Types 8 → 2 → 4

At each type number:
- Feel the energy beneath your feet.
- Ask your question.
- Speak your response out loud.
Don't rush. Let each number offer something.

TIP
Your question may shift naturally along the way. That's totally fine – just stay connected to what feels true in the moment.

Step 7: Return to Type 1

Back where you started. Take a breath. Let the entire experience integrate. Ask: *What have I learned through this process?* Say it aloud.

PART 3 WHAT AM I MOVING TOWARD?

PROCESS #5: HEXAD DIRECTION 2 (WITH THE ARROWS)
1 → 4 → 2 → 8 → 5 → 7 → 1
A 7-Step Process for Awareness, Introspection, and Growth
Use this process when participants want to explore...
Extra insight on a situation
Unspoken or unresolved elements
Areas of curiosity and intuition

Step 1: Start at Type 1
Stand at Type 1. Ground yourself. Feel your feet on the map and the energy of Type 1. Ask your question out loud. Speak the answer as it arises.

Step 2: Move to Type 4
Walk along the arrow line to Type 4. Take your time. Once you arrive, ask the same question again. Speak the answer out loud.

Step 3: Move to Type 2
Walk slowly along the arrow line from Type 4 to Type 2. Stand still. Ask your question and share the insights.

> **TIP**
> Always walk on the actual arrow lines slowly and mindfully. Pay attention to how the energy changes between types. It matters.

Steps 4 – 6: Continue the process for the following sequence: Types 8 → 5 → 7
At each type number:
Feel the energy beneath your feet.
Ask your question.
Speak your response out loud.
Don't rush. Let each number offer something.

> **TIP**
> Your question may shift naturally along the way. That's totally fine – just stay connected to what feels true in the moment.

Step 7: Return to Type 1
Back where you started. Take a breath. Let the entire experience integrate.
Ask: *What have I learned through this process?* Say it aloud.

PART 3 WHAT AM I MOVING TOWARD?

PROCESS #6: CENTERS OF INTELLIGENCE: HEAD (INSIGHT, CLARITY), HEART (RELATIONSHIPS, FEELINGS), BODY (TRUTH, ACTION)
A 4-Step Process for Achieving Wholeness
Use this process when participants want to explore...
Uncertainty and confusion
Multiple perspectives
Integration of thought, feeling and action

Step 1: Start at any Center you choose
Stand at that Center with your body directly over the core type of that Center: Type 6 for the Head Center, Type 3 for the Heart Center, and Type 9 for the Body Center. Make sure that your feet are standing on the types on either side the Center's core type. For example, if you are at the Body Center, put your right foot on Type 8, your left foot on Type 1, and have your body on top of Type 9. Take a moment to experience that Center somatically – feel the energy under your feet. Ask the question you want answered. Let the answer arise and speak it aloud. Keep speaking as long as responses continue to come.

> **TIP**
> Encourage specificity in the questions. General questions get general answers.

Step 2: Move to another Center
Walk the rim of the Enneagram circle to get to the next Center of Intelligence. Walk slowly and with intention – feel the shift in energy. Once you arrive at the new Center, position yourself with your body over the core type for the Center and one foot on the other types of that Center. Take a moment to experience that Center somatically – feel the energy under your feet. Ask the question. Let the answer emerge and speak it aloud.

PART 3 WHAT AM I MOVING TOWARD?

Step 3: Move to another Center
Walk the rim of the Enneagram circle to get to the next Center of Intelligence. Walk slowly and with intention - feel the shift in energy. Once you arrive at the new Center, position yourself with your body over the core type for the Center and one foot on the other types of that Center. Take a moment to experience that Center somatically - feel the energy under your feet. Ask the question. Let the answer emerge and speak it aloud.

TIP
Your question may shift naturally along the way. That's totally fine - just stay connected to what feels true in the moment.

Step 4: Move to the center of the Enneagram symbol
Breathe, experience what being in the center of the symbol is like. Let everything integrate. Say whatever emerges aloud.

Extra: Ask the map for guidance in terms of the affirming force for your development desires: *What do I want?* You can use the map to identify what you want or to deepen your understanding of a "want" you think you have. Maybe you want it more than you realized or a for a different reason. Maybe it wasn't what you really wanted at all. Exploring what you want through the Centers of Intelligence offers deep insight and also helps identify conflicting desires that may exist.

Notes

PART 3 WHAT AM I MOVING TOWARD?

AWARENESS, EXPLORATION AND PRACTICE

Whatever development path you choose, it always involves a three-step process: awareness, exploration and practice.

Awareness: the ability to see yourself clearly and in real time, recognizing your thoughts, emotions, behaviors, motivations, and impact on others without immediately reacting, defending, or changing anything. It forms the foundation for any meaningful development. Without awareness, you're on autopilot.

Exploration: the active, curious, and often non-linear process of discovering more about yourself. It lies between awareness and practice, where awareness sheds light, exploration navigates the terrain, and practice builds the muscle.

Practice: the deliberate, repeated application of new awareness and insights in everyday life. It's where growth becomes embodied and integrated, not just understood conceptually.

Which part of this 3-step process do you tend to do more of and which less of?

How are your answers connected to your Enneagram type?

To what extent does your preference for one step of this process help and hinder your growth?

PART 3 WHAT AM I MOVING TOWARD?

AWARENESS

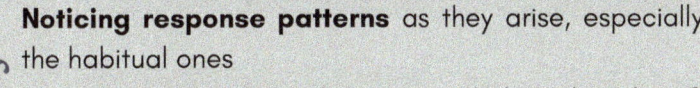

Awareness involves five sequential, yet distinct, factors:

- **Noticing response patterns** as they arise, especially the habitual ones
- **Recognizing internal states** including thoughts, feelings, and physical sensations
- **Being conscious of your impact** on yourself, others, and your environment
- **Witnessing without judgment** as a neutral observer
- **Seeing the gap** between your current self and your idealized self

There are many activities available that heighten self-awareness, and many of them are fun to do as well as enlightening. Here are six activities for you to use that increase your awareness. Please remember that almost anything you do can expand your awareness if you do it from a place of "presence."

MINDFUL SELF-OBSERVATION

Pause in real time, then breathe, ask the question, reflect, then answer.

Level 1

What are my thoughts?

What am I feeling?

What parts of my body can I sense?

Level 2

What are the patterns or themes of my thoughts?

Which of these feelings are highly familiar to me?

As I slowly scan my body, what familiar sensations do I experience somatically?

Mindful Self-Observation

PART 3 WHAT AM I MOVING TOWARD?

MINDFUL SELF-OBSERVATION (CONTINUED)

Level 3

What are my meta-level thoughts, the beliefs behind my thought patterns?

What am I feeling now that is related to my deeper emotional patterns?

What is my body telling me now that I really need to listen to?

PATTERN MAPPING

Step 1: Draw your patterns. Words are fine, yet you can go beyond words to show the relationships between the items on your map. This takes your understanding to a deeper level.

Pattern Mapping

Step 2: Reflect on what triggers your patterns

What triggers your positive and negative patterns?

PART 3 WHAT AM I MOVING TOWARD?

PATTERN-MAPPING (CONTINUED)

Step 3: Identify what triggers your triggers
For each of your selected triggers, what triggers or ignites each of them? List these.

Step 4: How do you respond when triggered?
When you get triggered in each of the areas selected, how do you actually behave or respond?

EMBODIED CHECK-INS

Have you ever done a full-body check-in as a way to invite awareness?

Step 1: Relax and breathe
Wherever you are, sitting or standing, take a relaxing breath through your nose and gently exhale through your mouth. Do this several times, then feel your feet where they touch the ground.

Step 2: Start with your feet
Starting with your feet, pay attention to what you notice about them touching the ground. Moving upward from your feet to your ankles, notice where you feel relaxed and where you experience tension. As you move upward through your legs and into the rest of your entire body, notice all of your sensations until you reach the top of your head.

Embodied Check-Ins

Step 3: Reflect on your experience
What was your experience doing an embodied check-in?

PART 3 WHAT AM I MOVING TOWARD?

SILENCE AND STILLNESS

Being silent and still involves the art of non-doing. Silence goes beyond not verbalizing. Silence also refers to silence in the mind with minimal to no mental chatter. Stillness often suggests the body and lack of visible movement, but this is just the beginning. Stillness also means a still mind, free of thoughts, and a still heart, one that is calm and relaxed.

Silence & Stillness

You can lie down, sit, stand or even walk in silence and stillness. Being silent and still takes attention and practice. What helps is intention and breath combined. If you make your intention to be silent and still and also focus your attention on your breath or breathing, becoming silent and still becomes easier.

In silence and stillness you can notice what usually goes unnoticed.

Reflect on your experience
Practice being silent and still; reflect on your experience with silence and stillness.

MIRRORED JOURNALING

In mirrored journaling, you write, you draw, you doodle, all without any judgment or censorship. You write with honesty, truthfulness, and full disclosure.

There's no audience so you don't write for one, and no one is going to read what you write unless you choose to share it. You write to tell your story without edits. You convey your narrative and if your narrative changes as you write, you can write your newer narrative.

Mirrored Journaling

PART 3 WHAT AM I MOVING TOWARD?

MIRRORED JOURNALING (CONTINUED)

To start, you simply just start writing and see what comes out of your pen or pencil with no pre-planning or formal structure. All you need is the intention to be true to yourself. It could be about you, others, your environment, or a dialogue between your current and younger self or your True Self (higher self) and False Self (ego). You get to decide.

No censoring, spelling doesn't matter, and you have plenty of room to write below:

PART 3 WHAT AM I MOVING TOWARD?

REAL-TIME REWIND

Awareness grows when we look backward to reflect on our experiences and reactions as a way to gain insight as we move forward.

Think of an experience that had a big impact on you, then answer these questions:

Real-Time Rewind

What did you think?

What did you feel?

What did you do?

What did you say?

What did you assume?

What did you avoid?

What did you embrace?

What did you learn?

PART 3 WHAT AM I MOVING TOWARD?

EXPLORATION

Exploration refers to the active, curious, and often non-linear process of discovering more about yourself. It sits between awareness and practice – where awareness shines the light, exploration walks the terrain, and practice builds the muscle. Exploration involves the following:

Curiosity about investigating your patterns, motivations, and reactions without judgment

Trying new perspectives by asking "What else could be true?" or "What would happen if I thought, felt or did this differently?"

Emotional risk-taking being willing to experience discomfort in service of growth – for example, by exploring fear, anger, or vulnerability rather than avoiding these responses

Learning through experience such as testing new behaviors, making different choices, trying different responses, or experimenting with new internal narratives

Discovering inner terrain by uncovering beliefs, values, habits, defense mechanisms, or shadow aspects that are usually outside your conscious awareness

Sitting with uncertainty or contradictions, allowing insight to emerge rather than forcing solutions

PURPOSEFUL DISRUPTION

To help you explore, here are three activities that can be illuminating. Try all of them!

Disrupt your natural patterns. Think of these as "low-hanging fruit" that are easy to see but still challenging to do. But you can do it. Try the one for your type on the following page or make up a disruption of your own. Explore this now, in real time, using this process:

The Process
Recognize the pattern
Intentionally disrupt it
    Stop it
    Replace it
See what emerges

Purposeful Disruption

PART 3 WHAT AM I MOVING TOWARD?

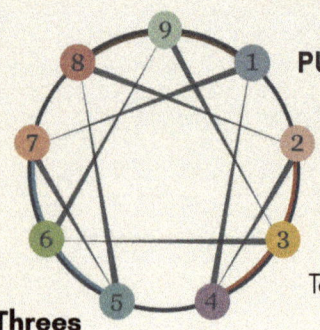

PURPOSEFUL DISRUPTION (CONTINUED)

You can try these type-based purposeful disruptions:

Ones
Make a mistake on purpose; experience it and enjoy it.

Twos
Talk without using your hands.

Threes
For a specific amount of time, do only what you want, not what you think you should do or should want.

Fours
Communicate without using words that reference yourself: *I, me, my, mine, myself*.

Fives
Converse with multiple other people and make sure your intention with all of them is to be emotionally transparent.

Sixes
Say "yes" with sincerity before you start thinking about how to solve a problem by running through your mental check-list of why something may not work.

Sevens
Stay with being bored for five minutes without distraction.

Eights
Experience being receptive by conversing using a softer and reflective tone.

Nines
Be the first person to speak up in a conversation.

Reflect on your experiences disrupting your type-based pattern.

PART 3 WHAT AM I MOVING TOWARD?

EXPRESS YOURSELF CREATIVELY

Paint, sculpt, sing, dance, create poetry from the place inside you that desires a new way of being, a new quality, or a different way of approaching something. Select something you want to explore, then select the medium or modality to express it. Finally, get creative. Alternatively, select your medium or modality first, then choose what you want to explore.

Express Yourself Creatively

Explore your creative expression here. Write a poem, jot down some ideas for some music or art you want to create.

PART 3 WHAT AM I MOVING TOWARD?

PERSPECTIVES

Select a situation in your life that confuses, perplexes, or distresses you. Explore how you are handling that situation including your thoughts, feelings, behaviors, and overall assessment or perspective on the situation. Now think about the other eight Enneagram types. Going type by type, ask yourself what their perspective on the situation would be, including thoughts, feelings and behavioral responses. After considering each type's perspective, ask yourself this: *What if I adopted this perspective? What would happen?* You can do this by writing down your responses here, on a separate piece of paper, or, if you have an Enneagram symbol floor map, you can stand on each type number to inquire about their perspective.

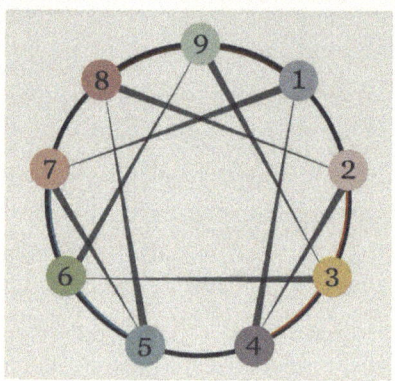

Perspectives

PART 3 WHAT AM I MOVING TOWARD?

PRACTICE

Practice refers to the intentional, repeated application of new awareness and insights in real time and real life so that growth becomes embodied and integrated, not just understood; it's "doing the thing," not just "knowing the thing," and is a spiral process not a linear one. Practice helps you do the following:

Turn insight into action by applying what you've explored – a new mindset, response, or behavior.

Build new habits by rewiring your default patterns through repetition and conscious choice.

Fail forward by accepting mistakes and missteps as part of the process. Practice isn't perfection – it's progress.

Make the uncomfortable familiar because practice reshapes your nervous system, your sense of self, and relational dynamics.

THE PRACTICE SPIRAL

1. Experiment (Try it!)
2. Experience (Don't hold back)
3. Examine (Reflect on your experience)
4. Enhance (Make adjustments)
5. Engage (Is this better?)

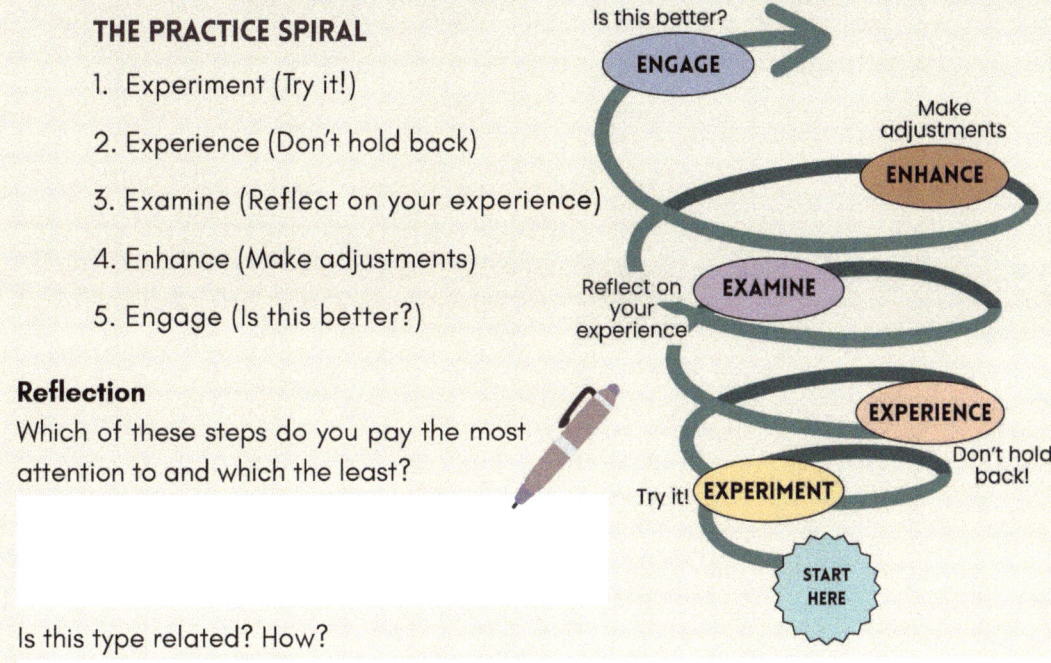

Reflection

Which of these steps do you pay the most attention to and which the least?

Is this type related? How?

What would happen if you paid more attention to the step that you pay the least attention to currently?

PART 3 WHAT AM I MOVING TOWARD?

DEVELOPMENT PATHWAYS

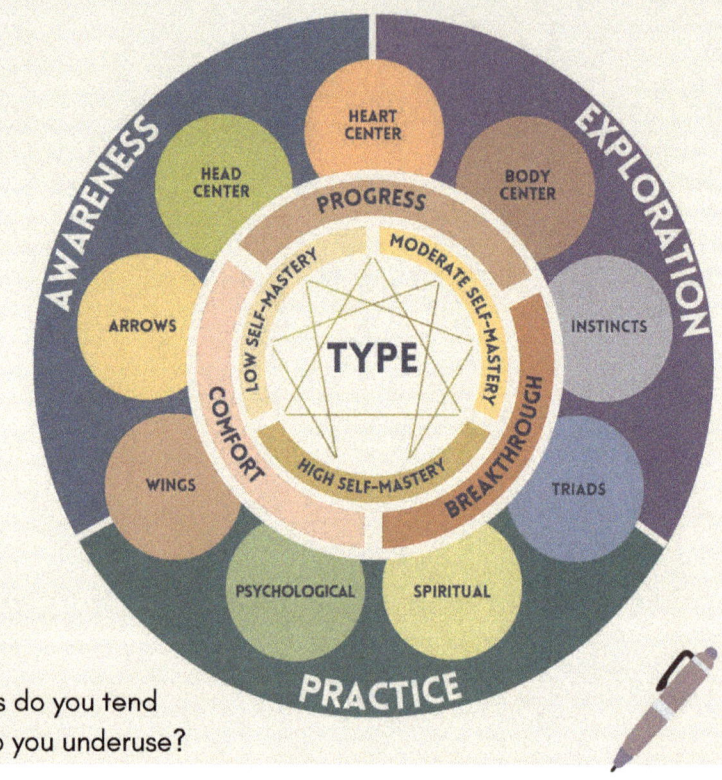

Reflection
Which development paths do you tend to use most and which do you underuse?

Given the kind of growth you want and your level of self-mastery, is this working well for you? If we get too comfortable, then we may not make much progress and certainly no breakthroughs.

Are you making the kind of development movement you most want?

PART 3 WHAT AM I MOVING TOWARD?

PART 3 HIGHLIGHTS

REMEMBER
There is power in the positive

Pursue what you love, value and desire, one development area at a time

Use multiple development paths

DO'S
Enjoy the process
Reward micro and macro changes
Be patient

DONT'S
Push or rush your growth
Sit in judgment; let it go
Justify yourself to anyone

REFLECTIONS

"Let yourself be silently drawn by the strange pull of what you really love. It will not lead you astray."
- Rumi

"Follow your bliss and the universe will open doors where there were only walls."
- Joseph Campbell

WHAT AM I MOVING AGAINST?

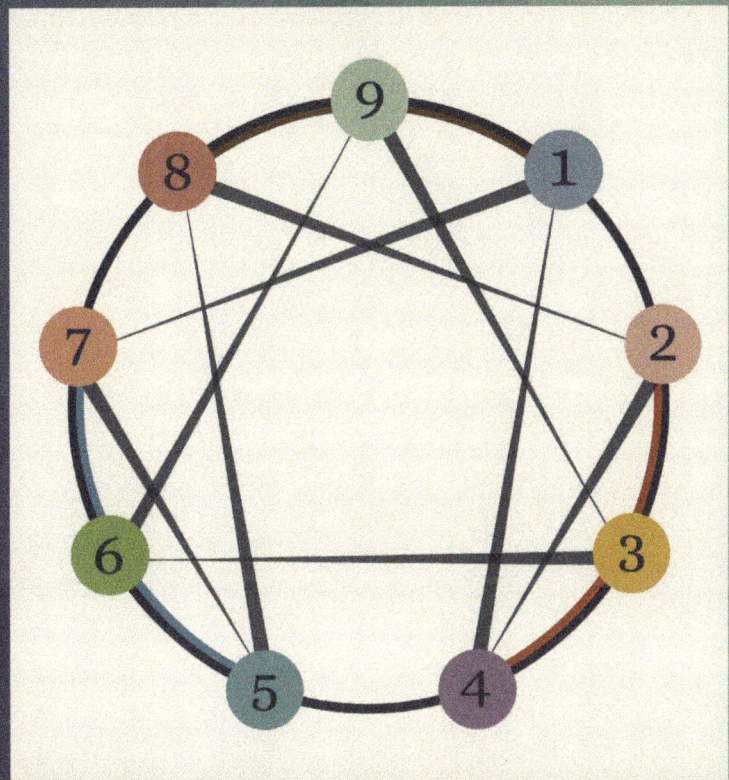

PART FOUR

PART 4: WHAT AM I MOVING AGAINST?
TABLE OF CONTENTS

Introduction	97
Three Forces of Transformation	98
11 Forms of Resistance	101
Shadow	105
Projection as Avoidance	107
Structure of Resistance	108
Shadow Work	119
Development Paths	128
Wings as Shadows	129
Highlights	130

INTRODUCTION

Simple changes can be achieved following the momentum of the affirming 1st force, but transformation requires the 2nd force, the denying force, to arise. That's because every affirming movement toward growth also evokes an equal pull in the opposite direction. This is not regression. It's this energy or forward momentum and the dynamic between these two forces – toward and against – that makes integration possible. This cautionary resisting force, the 2nd force, creates invaluable restraint, opposition and a different kind of vibrant energy.

The focus now moves from the affirming force in Part 3 to Part 4, which explores this 2nd force, the denying force that we often try to submerge or avoid, which often shows up as resistance. This force can be painful, challenging, and difficult, but it is also essential for change and transformation. The 2nd force has many forms, but one of them can be resistance. Here you can explore the 11 faces of resistance, their connection to the Enneagram types, plus the shadow elements of each Enneagram type and how to shine the light on them.

Did you know that there's a predictable structure of resistance for each Enneagram type or that one of the ways to understand our Enneagram-type wings is as shadows of our type? All of this and more are in Part 4.

PART 4 WHAT AM I MOVING AGAINST?

THREE FORCES OF TRANSFORMATION

GURDJIEFF'S LAW OF THREE

Simple change only requires the energy of the affirming force (wanting something) or the denying force (avoiding something). Transformation, however, requires the dynamic energy of all three forces: the affirming force, the denying force, and the reconciling force.

When it comes to our development, some of us want to refrain from focusing on the areas we prefer to avoid. This doesn't actually work effectively, even if it feels more comfortable. Real transformation requires all three forces to be activated.

RECONCILING
THIRD FORCE
INTEGRATES AND TRANSFORMS

PUSHES BACK

INITIATES CHANGE

DENYING
SECOND FORCE

AFFIRMING
FIRST FORCE

Think of a time when you experienced a transformation. What were the affirming forces involved?

The denying forces?

What was the reconciling force?

How did you experience each of these forces somatically and energetically? Use words to describe your experience being in each of these three states.

PART 4 WHAT AM I MOVING AGAINST?

THREE FORCES OF TRANSFORMATION (CONTINUED)

Our True Self doesn't emerge from the affirming force only; using only the affirming energetic force can easily lead to psychological and/or spiritual bypassing. On the other hand, the denying force by itself makes us smaller and despairing.

Our True Self emerges from the dynamic interplay between the affirming, denying and reconciling forces.

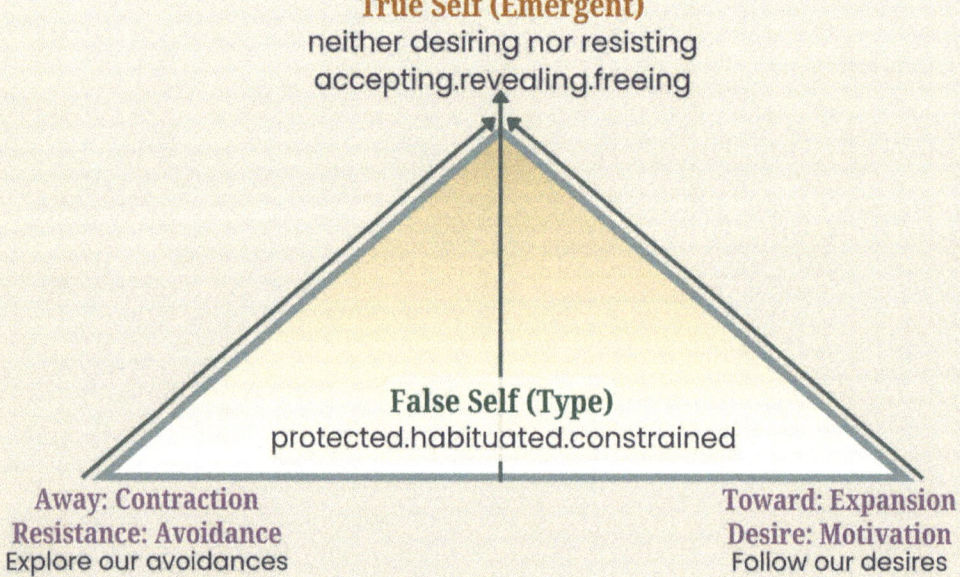

When have you experienced the forces of contraction and expansion, avoidance and desire, operating within you?

Have you ever experienced a third, reconciling force in these situations and, if so, what was the result?

PART 4 WHAT AM I MOVING AGAINST?

RESISTANCE

Resistance is a natural part of self-development work. It's not the enemy of growth; it's a signal that something is in our shadow: an unresolved fear, a challenge to our self-image or ego structure, a past trauma, socialized belief systems, or something else. Resistance appears as a way to protect, preserve, or prevent something, but what? The key is learning how to work with resistance, not to fight against it.

Resistance is layered

Surface resistance might sound like: *I'm too busy* or *This isn't the right time*.

But, a deeper look often reveals fears like: *Who will I be without this pattern? If I accept something as true about myself, my sense of self is at risk. If I don't resist this, something terrible might occur.*

Deeper still lie unresolved issues – emotional, past experiences, socialized belief systems, etc.

Resistance can intensify when we are on the verge of a breakthrough.

Force doesn't work with resistance; force intensifies resistance.
The antidote to force is curiosity, compassion, and a slower pace.

How do I know when I am triggered, resisting, or avoiding something?

How do I respond when I am triggered?

What does my body experience when I am triggered?

How do I unconsciously leak my discomfort (in other words, I am upset but avoid expressing it directly)?

PART 4 WHAT AM I MOVING AGAINST?

11 FORMS OF RESISTANCE

We all use different forms of resistance, but certain Enneagram types may use some forms more than others. But, underneath all resistance is a shadow to work with.

Denial Minimizing or completely ignoring what needs attention

Anger Using different forms of anger, from rage to irritation and frustration, as a cover

Rationalization Justifying the avoidance with excuses and seemingly logical reasons

Procrastination Delaying what needs to be done or avoiding it entirely

Distraction Constantly shifting focus to avoid sitting with discomfort or self-reflection

Cynicism Using sarcasm, dismissal, or intellectual superiority to avoid vulnerability

Withholding Holding back thoughts, feelings, or action - especially in relationships or group settings

Perfectionism Avoiding action until it can be done exactly "right"

Blaming Projecting discomfort, blockages and responsibility onto others

Tuning out Numbing out through distractions, overconsumption, or disconnecting from self and others

Over-efforting Trying too hard and working too long as a way to avoid inner stillness or vulnerability

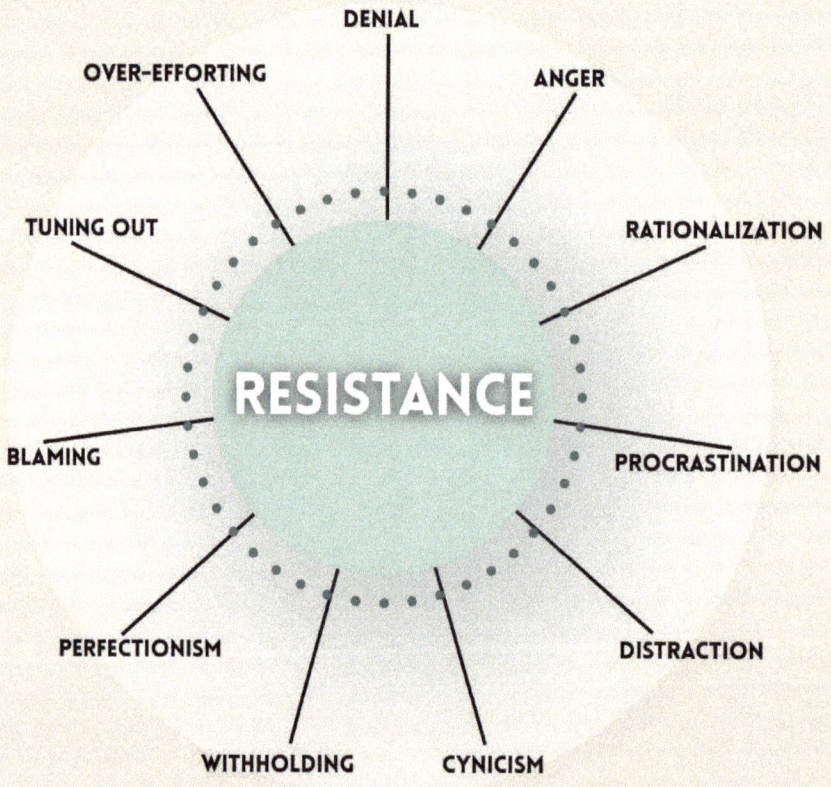

PART 4 WHAT AM I MOVING AGAINST?

Which forms of resistance do you most often use?

How does this form of resistance relate to your Enneagram type?

DEALING WITH RESISTANCE EFFECTIVELY

Once we can identify our resistance in real-time, we can choose to do something instead of resisting. Knowing your most frequently used forms of resistance can help you select in advance alternative behaviors that help you reduce or even eliminate your resistance.

Review the forms of resistance and next to each one, check the alternative response or responses you are willing to explore.

Denial Minimizing or completely ignoring what needs attention

What to do instead

- [ ] Review feedback related to recurring patterns in your life
- [ ] Work with a trusted guide, coach, or friend to increase self-honesty
- [ ] Inquire: "What am I not seeing that really needs attention?"

Anger Using different forms of anger, from rage to irritation and frustration, as a cover

What to do instead

- [ ] Name and normalize the anger: "This is my resistance showing up"
- [ ] Engage the body: Use movement, breathwork, or grounding techniques
- [ ] Inquire: "What am I protecting myself from feeling?"

PART 4 WHAT AM I MOVING AGAINST?

Rationalization Justifying the avoidance with excuses and seemingly logical reasons

What to do instead

- [ ] Use a reflection journal to challenge your internal excuses
- [ ] Engage a coach or peer to ask questions or give you feedback about this pattern
- [ ] Inquire: "What feelings, including fear, are hiding underneath this logic?"

Procrastination Delaying what needs to be done or avoiding it entirely

What to do instead

- [ ] Break tasks into smaller, manageable steps
- [ ] Use intermittent, pre-scheduled time blocks for self-care (15-minute walks, food breaks, meditations, etc.)
- [ ] Inquire: "What am I avoiding by delaying?"

Distraction Constantly shifting focus to avoid sitting with discomfort or self-reflection

What to do instead

- [ ] Designate specific, yet brief, times for stillness and inward focus
- [ ] Limit or remove common distraction sources
- [ ] Inquire: "What am I afraid I'll feel or experience in the silence?"

Cynicism Using sarcasm, dismissal, or intellectual superiority to avoid vulnerability

What to do instead

- [ ] Reconnect with your original hopes and aspirational motivations
- [ ] Balance critique with a curiosity-mindset
- [ ] Inquire: "What pain or disappointment am I protecting myself from?"

Withholding Holding back thoughts, feelings, or action – especially in relationships or group settings

What to do instead

- [ ] Practice honest self-expression in safe spaces
- [ ] Share one truth at a time, even if it's small
- [ ] Inquire: "What do I fear will happen if I tell the truth?"

PART 4 WHAT AM I MOVING AGAINST?

Perfectionism Avoiding action until it can be done exactly "right"

What to do instead

- [ ] Practice intentional imperfect behaviors
- [ ] Track small wins instead of flawless outcomes
- [ ] Inquire: "Is it more important to be right than effective?"

Blaming Projecting discomfort, blockages and responsibility onto others

What to do instead

- [ ] Explore what the blame might be protecting (i.e., shame, fear)
- [ ] Examine what you may be projecting onto others
- [ ] Inquire: "What's my part in this situation?"

Tuning out Numbing out through distractions, specific behavior, overconsumption, or disconnecting from self and others

What to do instead

- [ ] Use mindfulness activities to anchor yourself (breath, body scan)
- [ ] Set boundaries on your use of technology or other distractions
- [ ] Inquire: "Why am I really doing this self-development work?"

Over-efforting Trying too hard and working too long as a way to avoid inner stillness or vulnerability

What to do instead

- [ ] Practice "non-doing" (rest, silence, spaciousness)
- [ ] Shift the focus from productivity to presence
- [ ] Inquire: "What am I afraid will happen if I stop?"

PART 4 WHAT AM I MOVING AGAINST?

SHADOW

The shadow is the part of ourselves we unconsciously reject, deny, or hide and includes traits, emotions, or desires we've learned are "bad," "wrong," or "unacceptable." The shadow isn't only negative. It also contains hidden strengths, creativity, and potential waiting to be reclaimed. Whatever the reason, when our shadow feels threatened in any way, we become resistant.

How do you feel about your shadow?

How do you feel about exploring your shadow more in depth?

PART 4 WHAT AM I MOVING AGAINST?

What do you think is in your shadow? Write down everything: qualities, skills, strengths, weakness and more. After you make a complete list, put a * next to each item you think relates to your Enneagram type in some way. Think of these as treasures or gifts you can re-integrate to help you become more whole.

What can you do to allow your shadow to become more illuminated?

PART 4 WHAT AM I MOVING AGAINST?

PROJECTION AS AVOIDANCE

One way we resist and avoid is through projection. We imagine that something that is actually true about us is about someone else. This is largely unconscious until we become more aware. What do you project onto others? Others are actually our mirrors, and we project onto them without recognizing this.

What Enneagram type do you like the best?
Write down that type number.

What qualities and attributes do they have that you like them so much? Make a list here.

Which Enneagram type do you like the least? Write down that type number.

What qualities and attributes do they have that you like them the least? Make that list here.

PART 4 WHAT AM I MOVING AGAINST?

Review both lists. How are these over-liked or under-liked qualities actually true about you?

What would happen if you re-owned or accepted the projected aspects of yourself and integrated them into your self-acceptance?

RESISTANCE

Did you know that there is a structure that resistance takes to protect our type-based ego structure and related ego ideal, our idealized self? Each Enneagram type has an ego ideal, a way we want to see ourselves and have others view us. Qualities and attributes that align with or confirm this ego ideal, we say, "Yes, that's me!" However, qualities and attributes that do not align with our type-based ego ideal we reject; they go into our "shadow," and we project these shadow elements onto others.

When our ego ideal feels threatened, our defense rises up, particularly the defense mechanism that is the primary defense for our Enneagram type. Then, our resistant behaviors emerge, with highly charged and type-specific causes underneath. And all of this is caused by a type-specific underlying fear.

It is important to understand our type-based resistance structures so we can identify them, relax them and gain access to what lies underneath for our development.

Here are the nine different structures of resistance. Most important for you to review is the structure of resistance for your Enneagram type. At the same time, reading the other eight resistance structures helps you understand the other Enneagram types better and to be able to compare and contrast with your type.

Note: Thanks to Jerry Wagner PhD for the type-based ego ideal names.

PART 4 WHAT AM I MOVING AGAINST?

STRUCTURE OF RESISTANCE TYPE ONE

Shadow
Anger, impulsiveness, self-indulgence, imperfection, hedonism, immorality, laziness, sensitivity

Type One Ego

Ego Ideal: The Good Person
Moral, hardworking, principled, responsible, organized, productive, consistent, quality-focused

Defense Mechanism: Reaction Formation
Reacting the opposite of their actual responses that they think are unacceptable

Resistant Behaviors
Become more angry and/or suppress anger, resist spontaneity, become more controlling, over-focus on details, judgments increase, become more rigid

Cause of Resistance
1s have a harsh internal inner critic ready to tell them when they have done something "wrong." As the Good Person, they have to be "good" or correct at all times. Admitting imperfection and mistakes is an affront to their idealized self and akin to a moral failure.

Underlying Fear
"If I relax my control and make any mistakes, will I become an irresponsible, wrong, and immoral person?"

PART 4 WHAT AM I MOVING AGAINST?

STRUCTURE OF RESISTANCE TYPE TWO

Shadow
Neediness, resentment, selfishness, boundaries, anger, intellectuality, withholding, manipulation

Type Two Ego

Ego Ideal: The Loving Person
Kind, thoughtful, generous, attuned, helpful, indispensable, nurturing, caring, compassionate

Defense Mechanism: Repression
Subduing and submerging feelings, personal needs, and desires

Resistant Behaviors
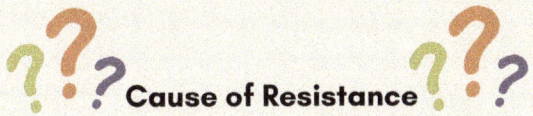
Avoid own needs, deflect attention from self by focusing on others, resist receiving, become agitated or angry, over-giving

Cause of Resistance
2s equate their value and self-worth with being affirmed for their kindness, thoughtfulness, selflessness and generosity. Acknowledging anything other than this in themselves is an affront to their idealized self as the Loving Person and makes them feel desperately unlovable.

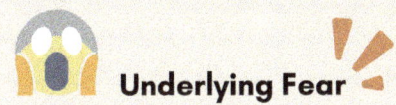
Underlying Fear
"If I'm needy or not completely available to others, will anyone still love me?"

PART 4 WHAT AM I MOVING AGAINST?

STRUCTURE OF RESISTANCE TYPE THREE

Shadow
Failure, deceit, emptiness, laziness, anxiety

Type Three Ego

Ego Ideal: The Effective Person
Competent, capable, productive, accomplished, successful, confident, professional, important

Defense Mechanism: Identification
Identify with an idealized image, role or activity, believing this is who they are

Resistant Behaviors
Overwork, constant activity, avoidance of emotions, especially feelings of failure or inadequacy, stoicism or outbursts of anger

Cause of Resistance
3s believe that their value comes solely from what they can achieve, accomplish and from being acknowledged and respected by others for their competence. Anything that challenges their idealized self as the Effective Person creates anxiety that they are a nobody.

Underlying Fear
"If I stop performing and achieving, will I still have value?"

PART 4 WHAT AM I MOVING AGAINST?

STRUCTURE OF RESISTANCE TYPE FOUR

Shadow
Envy, ordinariness, joy, steadiness, deeper feelings, self-acceptance

Type Four Ego

Ego Ideal: The Original Person
Creative, deep, sensitive, intense, special, unique, authentic, classy, different, intuitive

Defense Mechanism: Introjection
Internalizing negative judgments and perceptions without discerning their accuracy

Resistant Behaviors
Amplify emotions or uniqueness, resist the ordinary or mundane, become tenacious and angry, withdrawn and non-communicative, or both

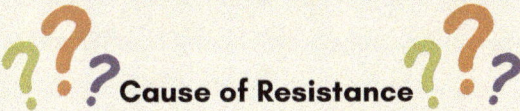

Cause of Resistance
4s believe that both their identity and value are tied to being unique and different and are highly sensitive to being rejected. Being intense, dramatic, finely tuned and deeply sensitive reinforces their idealized self as the Original Person, someone unlike any other and is a hedge against feelings of rejection.

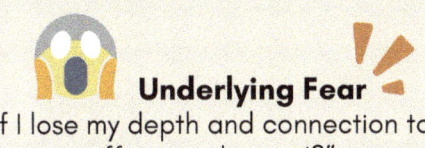

Underlying Fear
"If I lose my depth and connection to suffering, who am I?"

PART 4 WHAT AM I MOVING AGAINST?

STRUCTURE OF RESISTANCE TYPE FIVE

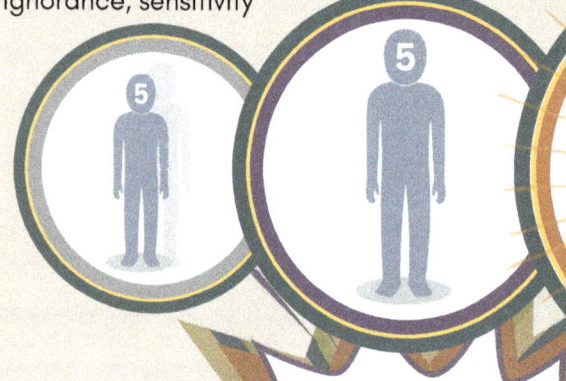

Shadow
Dependency, emotionality, needs, intrusion, ignorance, sensitivity

Type Five Ego

Ego Ideal: The Wise Person
Knowledgeable, observant, intellectual, complex, independent, non-emotional, private, autonomous

Defense Mechanism: Compartmentalization
Separation from the world, isolating thoughts from feelings, retreating into the mind

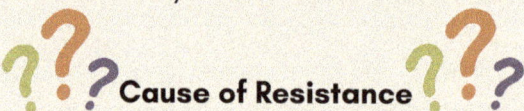

Resistant Behaviors
Withdraw, intellectualize, resist emotional exposure or any dependence, become heavily boundaried and adamant

Cause of Resistance
5s believe that all resources are scarce or limited, including their own time, energy and ability to stay present for emotional interactions. To deal with this fear of emotional overwhelm and utter depletion, they retreat into their minds where they feel safe and can sustain their idealized self as the Wise Person, someone of knowledge and insight. Any challenges to this meets fierce resistance.

Underlying Fear
"If I offer myself and my resources to others, will I be totally drained, like a near death experience?"

PART 4 WHAT AM I MOVING AGAINST?

STRUCTURE OF RESISTANCE TYPE SIX

Shadow
Authority, anger, inner knowing, defiance, recklessness, rebellion, inconsistency

Type Six Ego

Ego Ideal: The Loyal Person
Trustworthy, reliable, curious, cooperative, inquisitive, sincere, consistent

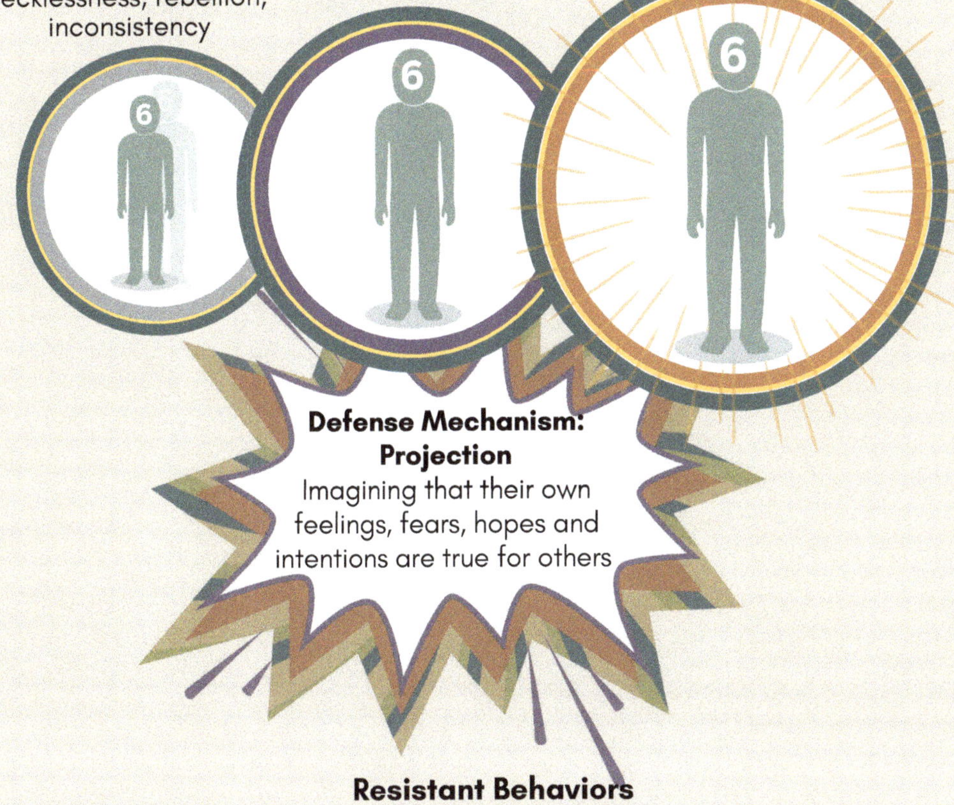

Defense Mechanism: Projection
Imagining that their own feelings, fears, hopes and intentions are true for others

Resistant Behaviors
Doubt self, accuse others, seek reinforcement for their thoughts, emotions, behavior and perspective, procrastinate, fight against what they imagine is occurring, project intensely onto others and situations, try to get other individuals and groups on their side

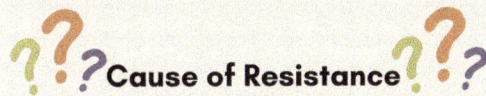

Cause of Resistance

Fear is the central emotion of all Head Center types and is also the 6's recurring emotional habit or passion. When 6s feel afraid, they resist. Their idealized self as the Loyal Person has them believe that their loyalty to people and institutions will keep them safe from their fears.

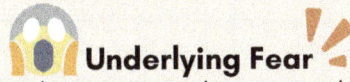

Underlying Fear

"If I trust myself and my own wisdom instead of seeking it from outside, will something terrible happen?"

PART 4 WHAT AM I MOVING AGAINST?

STRUCTURE OF RESISTANCE TYPE SEVEN

Shadow
Pain, limits, boredom, depth, pessimism, fear, seriousness

Type Seven Ego

Ego Ideal: The Joyful Person
Optimistic, enthusiastic, spontaneous, inventive, experimental, light-hearted, hopeful, engaging, fun-loving

Defense Mechanism: Rationalization
Reframing pain or anything negative as something positive

Resistant Behaviors
Escapism, continuous positive reframing, constantly moving mentally and physically, not adhering to any limits, anger if no exit is available

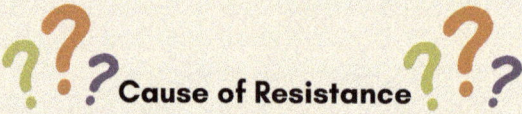

Cause of Resistance
7s avoid and resist anything and everything that they think will take them away from pleasure, stimulation, new ventures, unlimited possibilities, and being the Joyful Person they want to be.

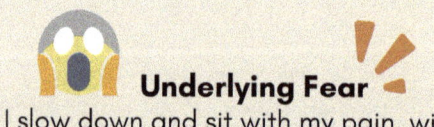

Underlying Fear
"If I slow down and sit with my pain, will I drown in my own discomfort?"

PART 4 WHAT AM I MOVING AGAINST?

STRUCTURE OF RESISTANCE TYPE EIGHT

Shadow
Vulnerability, tenderness, dependence, fear, indecision, weakness

Type Eight Ego

Ego Ideal: The Powerful Person
Independent, forceful, strong, courageous, assertive, protective, decisive

Defense Mechanism: Denial
Entirely eliminating anything that hurts them or makes them feel vulnerable

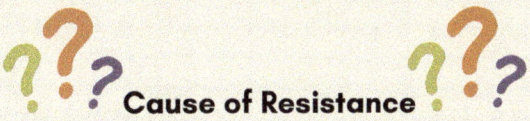

Resistant Behaviors
Invulnerable, highly controlling, blaming, non-receptive, immovable, emotionally defended, withdrawn, aggressive or both

Cause of Resistance
8s believe they have to stay armored up at almost all times in order to stay in charge, direct the action, control the big picture, be available to save the day and protect others. Thus, they resist anything that makes them feel vulnerable, dependent or weak and do what they need to do to maintain their ego ideal as the Powerful Person.

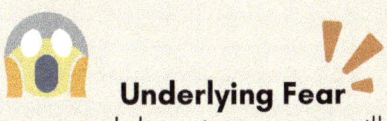

Underlying Fear
"If I let my guard down in any way, will I lose my power and control and be betrayed?"

PART 4 WHAT AM I MOVING AGAINST?

STRUCTURE OF RESISTANCE TYPE NINE

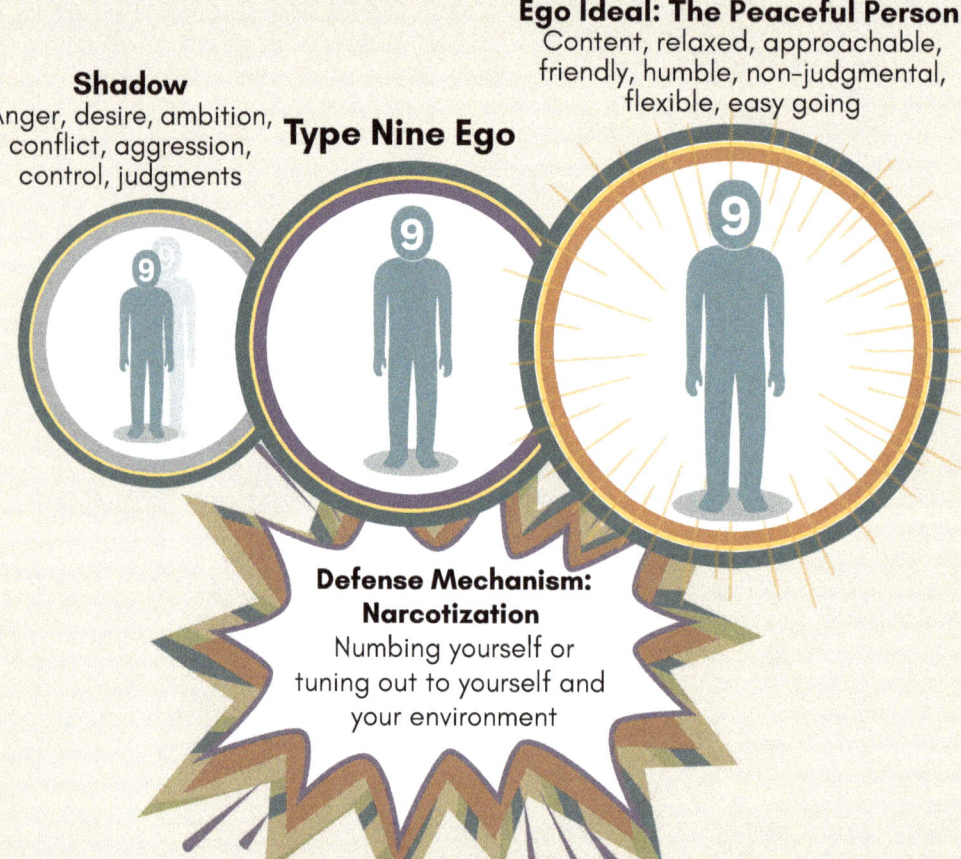

Shadow
Anger, desire, ambition, conflict, aggression, control, judgments

Type Nine Ego

Ego Ideal: The Peaceful Person
Content, relaxed, approachable, friendly, humble, non-judgmental, flexible, easy going

Defense Mechanism: Narcotization
Numbing yourself or tuning out to yourself and your environment

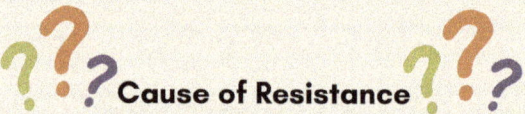

Resistant Behaviors
Being inattentive, sleeping, passive aggressiveness, increased merging with people, objects and routines, stubbornness

Cause of Resistance
9s believe that the ideal world is one of maximum peace and minimum tension and conflict. They keep the peace by not asserting themselves, merge and blend with others, control their desires and aspirations, and mediate when conflict arises. All this maintains their ego ideal as the Peaceful Person.

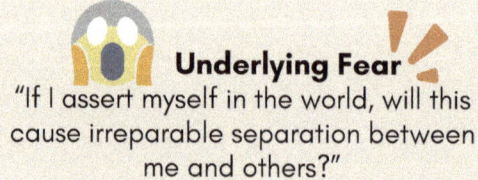

Underlying Fear
"If I assert myself in the world, will this cause irreparable separation between me and others?"

PART 4 WHAT AM I MOVING AGAINST?

STRUCTURE OF RESISTANCE REFLECTION

In what ways does the structure of resistance for your Enneagram type make sense to you?

What are the most important parts of your resistance structure for you to remember and focus on as you work on your deeper development?

PART 4 WHAT AM I MOVING AGAINST?

SHADOW WORK

Our shadow refers to unacknowledged, disowned, or repressed aspects of ourselves, often the opposite qualities of our idealized self, that stay in the dark until we shine the light on them.

Review the three shadow issues, two shadow practices, and the mantra for your type.

SHADOW WORK BY ENNEAGRAM TYPE

Enneagram Type One

Shadow issues
Messiness, pleasure seeking, rule breaking

Shadow practices

Allow yourself to feel your anger without judging it or renaming it so as to minimize it – for example, as irritation or frustration.

Practice spontaneity, which may require you to break some rules.

Mantra to repeat: *I can be messy, self-indulgent and still be good.*

Which of the three shadow issues is the most challenging for you to see in yourself?

What makes this such a challenge?

Which of the shadow practices offer you the most benefit?

What will it require of you to engage in this shadow practice?

PART 4 WHAT AM I MOVING AGAINST?
SHADOW WORK BY ENNEAGRAM TYPE

Enneagram Type Two

Shadow issues
Autonomy, self-interest, ambition

Shadow practices

Ask for something you want without offering anything in return.

Say no without needing to justify yourself to yourself or anyone else.

Mantra to repeat: *I can be selfish and still be lovable.*

Which of the three shadow issues is the most challenging for you to see in yourself?

What makes this such a challenge?

Which of the shadow practices offer you the most benefit?

What will it require of you to engage in this shadow practice?

PART 4 WHAT AM I MOVING AGAINST?
SHADOW WORK BY ENNEAGRAM TYPE

Enneagram Type Three

Shadow issues
Insecurity, authentic self-expression, vulnerability

Shadow practices
   Admit when you don't know, don't care, or don't want to do something or perform.

   Let yourself rest without feeling you need to earn something like respect, status, or the right to be in the roles with which you most identify.

   Mantra to repeat: *I can be ordinary and still have value.*

Which of the three shadow issues is the most challenging for you to see in yourself?

What makes this such a challenge?

Which of the shadow practices offer you the most benefit?

What will it require of you to engage in this shadow practice?

PART 4 WHAT AM I MOVING AGAINST?
SHADOW WORK BY ENNEAGRAM TYPE

Enneagram Type Four

Shadow issues

Deeper emotions beneath feelings, bitterness, playfulness

Shadow practices

Appreciate moments of contentment without dramatizing them.

Embrace simplicity and structure.

Mantra to repeat: *I can be balanced and grounded and still be deeply myself.*

Which of the three shadow issues is the most challenging for you to see in yourself?

What makes this such a challenge?

Which of the shadow practices offer you the most benefit?

What will it require of you to engage in this shadow practice?

PART 4 WHAT AM I MOVING AGAINST? SHADOW WORK BY ENNEAGRAM TYPE

Enneagram Type Five

Shadow issues
Secret life, longing for connection, sensitivity

Shadow practices
- Share a vulnerability in real time without practicing how to do it.
- Ask for help or emotional support.
- Mantra to repeat: *I can need others and ask for resources and still be capable.*

Which of the three shadow issues is the most challenging for you to see in yourself?

What makes this such a challenge?

Which of the shadow practices offer you the most benefit?

What will it require of you to engage in this shadow practice?

PART 4 WHAT AM I MOVING AGAINST?
SHADOW WORK BY ENNEAGRAM TYPE

Enneagram Type Six

Shadow issues
Aggression, disloyalty, guilt

Shadow practices
Challenge your own fears out loud.

Try doing the opposite of your usual plan.

Mantra to repeat: *I can feel uncertain and still trust myself.*

Which of the three shadow issues is the most challenging for you to see in yourself?

What makes this such a challenge?

Which of the shadow practices offer you the most benefit?

What will it require of you to engage in this shadow practice?

PART 4 WHAT AM I MOVING AGAINST? SHADOW WORK BY ENNEAGRAM TYPE

Enneagram Type Seven

Shadow issues
Wisdom, solitude, stillness

Shadow practices

Sit with discomfort and name it without trying to escape.

Reflect daily on one loss or regret.

Mantra to repeat: *I can be still and sad and also be fine.*

Which of the three shadow issues is the most challenging for you to see in yourself?

What makes this such a challenge?

Which of the shadow practices offer you the most benefit?

What will it require of you to engage in this shadow practice?

PART 4 WHAT AM I MOVING AGAINST?
SHADOW WORK BY ENNEAGRAM TYPE

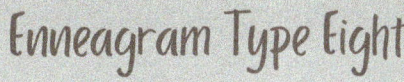 

Enneagram Type Eight

Shadow issues
Gentleness, innocence, intellectuality

Shadow practices
Reveal a fear or insecurity to someone you trust.

Let someone else lead or take care of you.

Mantra to repeat: *I can be soft and still be strong.*

Which of the three shadow issues is the most challenging for you to see in yourself?

What makes this such a challenge?

Which of the shadow practices offer you the most benefit?

What will it require of you to engage in this shadow practice?

PART 4 WHAT AM I MOVING AGAINST? SHADOW WORK BY ENNEAGRAM TYPE

Enneagram Type Nine

Shadow issues
Arrogance, being disruptive, self-orientation

Shadow practices
Let your desires lead instead of blending in with others.

Express a strong opinion – even if it causes tension.

Mantra to repeat: *I can disrupt the peace and still be in connection.*

Which of the three shadow issues is the most challenging for you to see in yourself?

What makes this such a challenge?

Which of the shadow practices offer you the most benefit?

What will it require of you to engage in this shadow practice?

PART 4 WHAT AM I MOVING AGAINST?

DEVELOPMENT PATHS

Are you choosing the best development paths? A path that works well for you may not be the best for others, even people of your same Enneagram type. Some paths work more effectively for certain development areas. Sometimes, we overuse one path and underuse another, just because that path is familiar to use and the other less so.

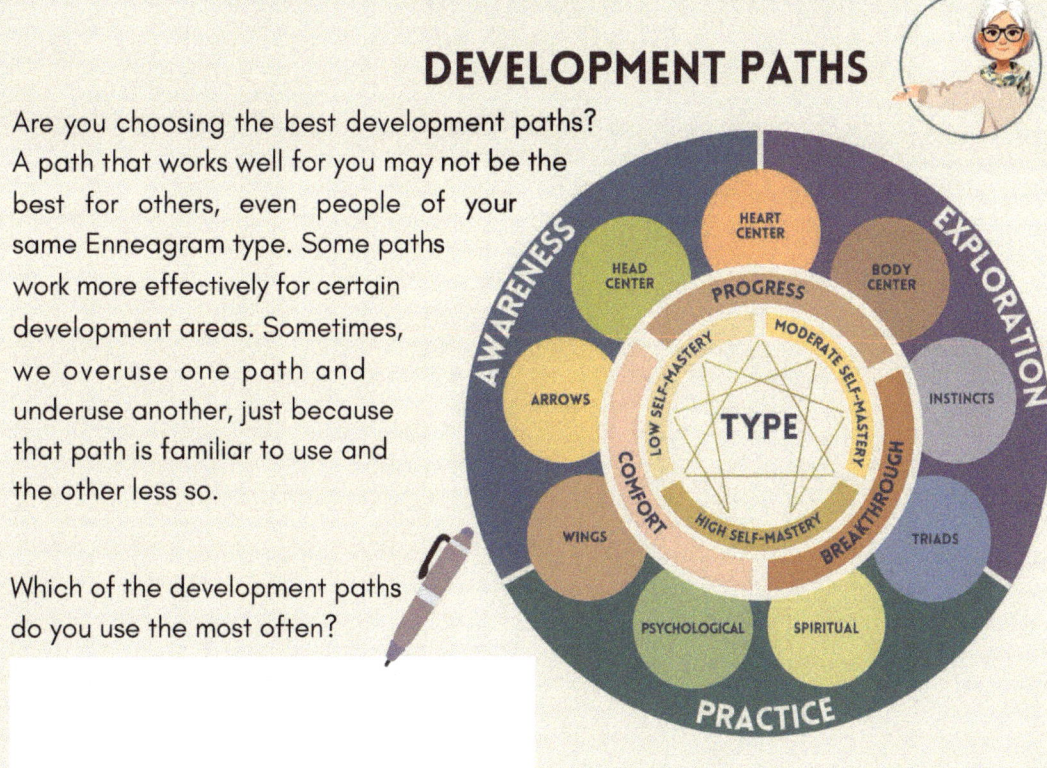

Which of the development paths do you use the most often?

Which of the development paths do you use the least often?

Does your choice of preferred paths relate to your Enneagram type? If so, how?

What kind of change do you want: comfort, progress or breakthrough?

How does your choice of development path(s) support your growth, given your type, your shadows or resistance behaviors, and the kind of change you want?

PART 4 WHAT AM I MOVING AGAINST?

WINGS AS SHADOWS

Remember that you can ask the map questions and elicit the wisdom of the Enneagram symbol as it combines with your own inner knowing. A large map on the floor is the best way to evoke answers to your questions, especially about insights that are in your shadow.

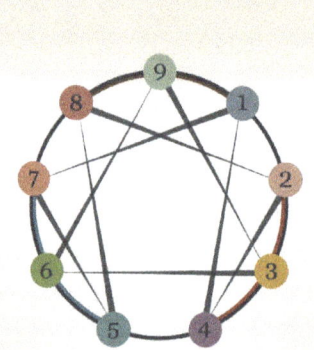

One theory that may be useful to you involves the wings for your type, the two types on either side of your core type. According to this theory, the type before your core type represents a shadow aspect of yourself that you first need to integrate into your current sense of self. Once this integration is done, the wing after your core type has some element(s) that need to be seen and integrated as you move into the future.

Try this theory out on the map:

Step 1: Begin at your type

Step 2: Move to the wing before your type
Ask this: *What do I need to see and integrate from you in order to be whole? How do I best do this?*

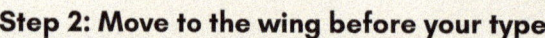

Step 3: Move back to your type
Breathe comfortably.

Step 4: Move to the other wing for your type
Ask this: *What do I need to see and integrate from you in order to grow into the future?*

What are some ways for me to do this?

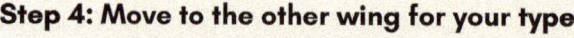

Step 5: Once there is an answer, move back to your type
Breathe gently. Feel free to ask the map any additional questions of your choice.

PART 4 WHAT AM I MOVING AGAINST?
PART 4 HIGHLIGHTS

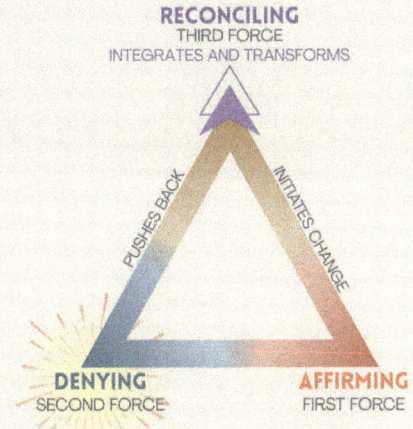

REMEMBER
Being resistant consumes a great amount of energy

Your shadow contains gifts and opportunities

Development paths you use less often may give you a stronger result

DO'S
Enjoy the process
Reward micro and macro changes
Be patient

DONT'S
Push or rush your growth
Judge or criticize yourself
Justify yourself to anyone

REFLECTIONS
"One does not become enlightened by imagining figures of light, but by making the darkness conscious."
- Carl Jung

"The cave you fear to enter holds the treasure you seek."
- Joseph Campbell

REACHING RECONCILIATION

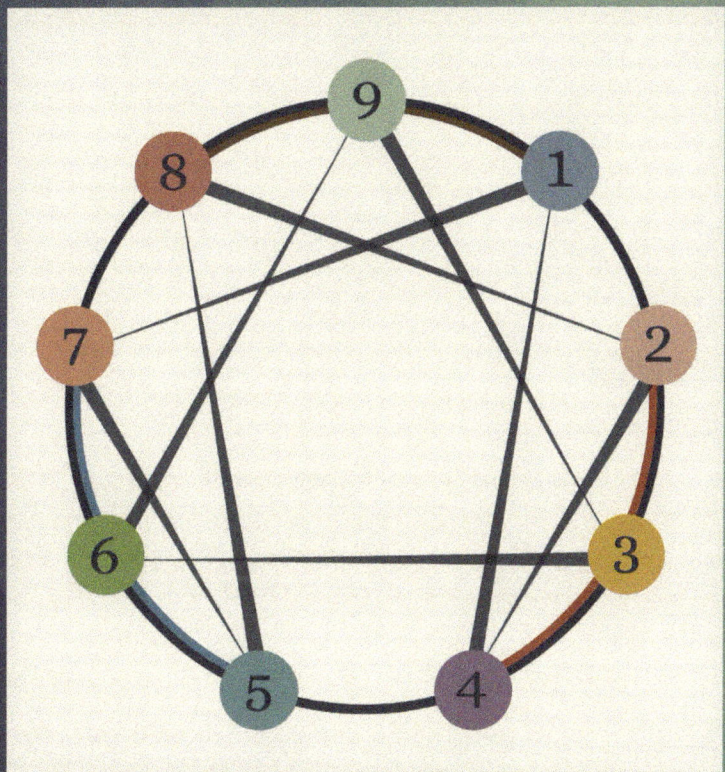

PART FIVE

PART 5: REACHING RECONCILIATION

TABLE OF CONTENTS

Introduction	133
5 Attributes of the 3rd Force	134
True Self and Law of Three	135
Centers of Intelligence and Law of Three	138
Centers of Intelligence and Wholeness	140
Opening Your Centers	141
Integrating Your Centers through Music	150
Arrows, Triads	151
Freeing the Instincts	167
Subtype-Based Development	180
Catalytic Conversions through Subtypes	199
Create Your Mandala	200
Highlights	203

INTRODUCTION

When what moves us forward meets what holds us back, a third force begins to stir, the possibility of reconciliation. Transformation requires all three energetic forces – 1st affirming, 2nd denying, and 3rd reconciling – to catalyze our development into integration and wholeness. With any one part missing, change can occur, but not transformation. The 1st force initiates the change, the 2nd forces pushes back against the change, and then the 3rd force emerges, reconciling and integrating the 1st and 2nd forces into a new and different whole.

Reconciliation isn't the end of tension; it's the ability to hold both the 1st and 2nd forces simultaneously and allow something new to appear.

PART 5 REACHING RECONCILIATION

FIVE ATTRIBUTES OF THE 3RD FORCE

Most of us are less familiar with the 3rd force, the energy of reconciliation and wholeness. These are the five main attributes of the 3rd force.

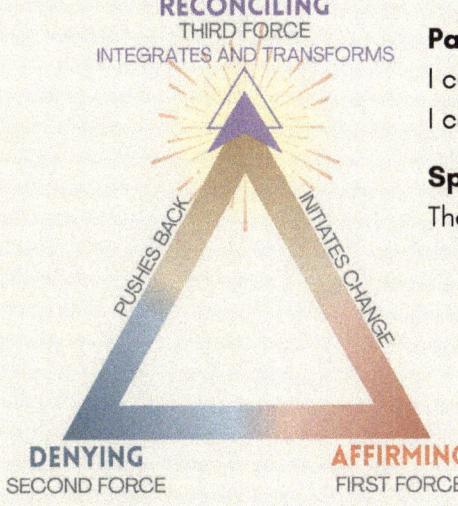

Paradox
I can get angry and still be a loving person.
I can be afraid and still take action.

Spaciousness
There's room for both affirming and denying forces.

Reframing
What if resistance is sacred?
What if moving toward something is limiting?

Creative pause
Something is not yet known; that's good.

Emergent wisdom
Something new is unfolding.

Are you more familiar with the affirming force or the denying force?

Are you familiar with the 3rd force, the reconciling force?

How do your answers relate to your Enneagram type?

PART 5 REACHING RECONCILIATION

TRUE SELF AND THE LAW OF THREE

It can be enlightening to understand how these three forces work together and particularly useful to explore their contribution to the emergence of our True Self. This illustration explains the forces, their energetics, their dynamic creativity, and how they lead to the emergence of the True Self.

RECONCILING FORCE (INTEGRATION/SYNTHESIS/WISDOM)
The superordinate 3rd force that holds paradox and catalyzes integration, not through compromise or dominance, but through fluidity, balancing and alignment

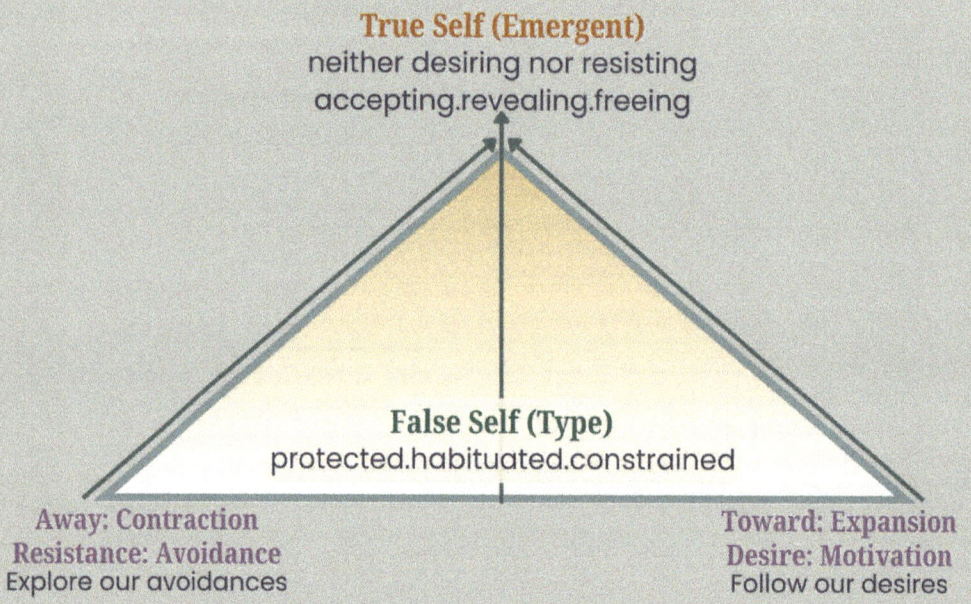

True Self (Emergent)
neither desiring nor resisting
accepting.revealing.freeing

False Self (Type)
protected.habituated.constrained

Away: Contraction
Resistance: Avoidance
Explore our avoidances

Toward: Expansion
Desire: Motivation
Follow our desires

COUNTERFORCE: DENYING
(RESISTANCE/STRUCTURE/DEFENSE)
The necessary counterbalance tests sincerity and slows unconscious action

FORCE: AFFIRMING
(CREATION/INITIATION/DESIRE)
The spark of growth, aspiration, or longing for something

PART 5 REACHING RECONCILIATION

Spend some time alone, reflecting on what you've learned about yourself: where you started in view of your self-mastery and psychological and spiritual development, what you've uncovered about where you want to grow and move toward, and also what you've been avoiding – perhaps something in your shadow. This is a time to take stock of where you are right now.

What is your most important development area right now?

What is causing you to move toward developing in this area (motivating you, affirming you to develop in that direction – the 1st force)?

What are the reasons why you avoid this development area (resistance areas, the questions or concerns – the 2nd force)?

How familiar or comfortable do you feel with the 3rd force, the reconciling energy? Is this new to you?

PART 5 REACHING RECONCILIATION

Take a time-travel journey, first to the past, then to the present, and finally to the future. Reflect on your journey from False Self to True Self.

PAST

Five years ago, where do you think you were on this journey? Place an X on the line from False Self to True Self.

Why did you place the X where you did?

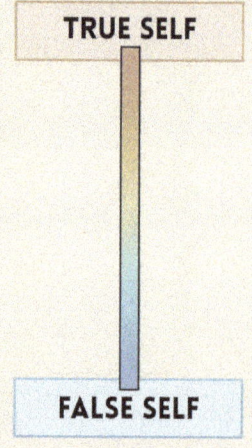

PRESENT

Currently, where do you think you are on this journey? Place an X on the line from False Self to True Self.

Why did you place the X where you did?

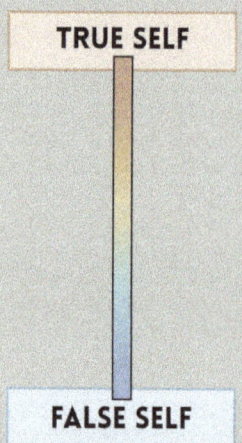

FUTURE

Five years from now, where do you want to be on this journey? Place an X on the line from False Self to True Self.

Why did you place the X where you did?

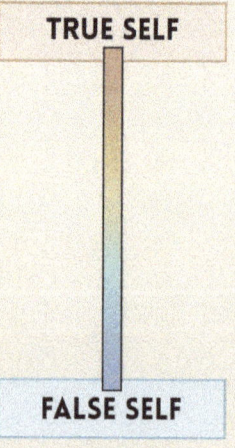

PART 5 REACHING RECONCILIATION

CENTERS OF INTELLIGENCE AND LAW OF THREE

The Enneagram symbol is made up of multiple triangles. Many of these triangles support transformational change using the Law of Three: affirming (1st force), denying (2nd force), and reconciling (3rd force). All three forces are not only needed, they are required for deep change to occur.

The three Centers of Intelligence can be used according to the Law of Three, with each Center capable of being used as any of these three transformative forces.

Center of Intelligence	Affirming Force Qualities	Denying Force Qualities	Reconciling Force Qualities
Head Center	Ideation, clarity, insight	Questioning, deep probing, scenario creation	Spaciousness, discernment, wisdom
Heart Center	Connection, compassion, values	Guilt, sorrow, rejection	Open-heartedness, self-acceptance, gratitude
Body Center	Action, forward movement, truth-telling	Control, discipline, tenacity	Presence, surrender, beingness

PART 5 REACHING RECONCILIATION

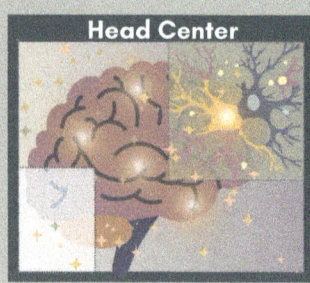
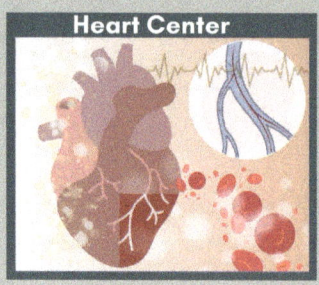
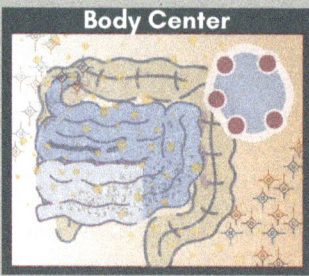

As you think about yourself, your Enneagram type, and your Centers of Intelligence, are you able to use all three Centers of Intelligence in all of the ways previously described?

How do you most commonly use each Center in terms of the three forces: affirming, denying, reconciling?

How is your answer connected to your Enneagram type, your level of self-mastery, and your overall psychological and spiritual development?

PART 5 REACHING RECONCILIATION

CENTERS OF INTELLIGENCE AND WHOLENESS

To use our three Centers of Intelligence to become more whole, we need to know what, why, and how.

Four Stages of Three-Centered Wholeness

This can be thought of as progress through the four stages of wholeness. In Stage One, the Centers need to be more balanced, while the challenge in Stage Two is to gain productive access to all three Centers. Stage Three involves integrating the Centers, while Stage Four is wholeness. In this stage, all three Centers are active and responsive, generating an embodied wisdom.

Wholeness — Responsive, wise, embodied 3-Centered presence in real time (STAGE FOUR)

Integrate — All three Centers collaborate productively in awareness and actions (STAGE THREE)

Rebalance — Recalibrate dominant Center for productive use; engage underused or misused Centers (STAGE TWO)

Imbalance — One Center over-active and dominating; other Centers suppressed or reactive (STAGE ONE)

Which of the four stages are you in?

What makes you think this?

What do you need to do to move from your current stage to the next higher stage?

> You can get additional insight and wisdom from your Centers of Intelligence using the Enneagram map process #6 described on page 79.

PART 5 REACHING RECONCILIATION

OPENING YOUR CENTERS

Have you wondered how to open more access to the productive uses of each Center of Intelligence?

There are specific ways for each type to open up access to each Center.

As you read the two suggested activities for each Center of Intelligence for your Enneagram type, put an X near the choice for each Center you think would help you the most. You will then have three actions you can pursue, one for opening each Center.

Enneagram Type One

Head Center Opening

☐ Go beyond the specific, immediate facts to the patterns implicit in the facts; understand the themes derived from these patterns. Doing this takes you beyond creating opinions based on initial thinking into understanding the bigger or deeper themes and issues.

☐ Make sure you don't over-plan decisions or over-organize your activities; allow room for new information to emerge. This helps you slow down your quick reaction time and also be more flexible and open to new information.

Heart Center Opening

☐ Be willing to explore and share deeply-held feelings when discussing issues, even if you feel uncomfortable doing so. The more you do this, the easier it becomes.

☐ You likely have a pattern of breathing into your abdomen and shoulder/head area, but less so into your heart. Practice also breathing into the heart and full torso each time you breathe. Over time, this will help open access to your Heart Center.

Body Center Opening

☐ Practice moving in a free form way to all different kinds of music. You don't have to be good at it or even look good. Just enjoy the freedom of moving your body in space without restriction.

☐ Learn to honor your somatic reactions by asking yourself what it is that you know very deeply to be true, with an emphasis on "know very deeply" rather than quick reactivity.

PART 5 REACHING RECONCILIATION

Head Center Opening

☐ Don't let your personal feelings and perceptions about situations and other people be your only compass; strive to be objective as well as subjective.

☐ Don't over-plan when you're anxious or under-plan when you're tired; be careful about overscheduling yourself because you think you must justify your existence by being there for other people.

Heart Center Opening

☐ Explore your deeper motivations for needing to know exactly what others are thinking and feeling. Focus more on yourself and ask this: *What am I thinking and feeling?* Asking and answering this question helps reduce your defense mechanism of repression and also opens up your heart.

☐ To open your Heart Center more means you need to be more receptive or open to receiving support and various forms of love from other people. You may be good at giving, but what about receiving?

Body Center Opening

☐ You may be motivated to support others and reduce their suffering as soon as you can. However, it is important for you to learn the art of timing so that you will know when to act, when to wait, and when to do nothing.

☐ Do you trust your somatic responses as much as you trust what your heart tells you? The body has its own wisdom, but you need to pay attention to it and know what it's communicating. Spend more time engaging in somatic activities like walking, being in nature, getting massages, exercising, martial arts, and dancing. When you feel a sensation in your body, ask yourself what this means in terms of your thinking, feeling, and sensing.

PART 5 REACHING RECONCILIATION

Enneagram Type Three

Head Center Opening

☐ Does your desire for effectiveness and efficiency, your attachment to goals and plans, and your need to do what you think you should do constrict your thinking so your mind becomes less agile and flexible? The less you go into mental lockdown on something, the more your Head Center opens. Relax your mind.

☐ Can you not know something, admit this to yourself and others, and then pursue the information without feeling anxious? Cultivate mental curiosity!

Heart Center Opening

☐ You likely use your emotional sensitivities to read your audience so you can adjust your behavior to make a more positive impression. Practice using your Heart Center to also tune into your own feelings and emotional experiences.

☐ Share your real feelings – including anxieties and sorrows – with others; this will help dismantle the overly confident image you have created that serves as an emotional barrier between you and others.

Body Center Opening

☐ Effective action isn't always fast action; sometimes it involves introspective deliberation, which can take more time. Experiment with taking action less quickly so that new insights and pathways have time to percolate. Try to balance your focus on results with attention to the process of getting the result.

☐ Become more aware of your body's signals. There is enormous wisdom in the body, but you have to understand the meaning of the signals. Your somatic reactions can help you work with your emotional responses, differentiate between what you really want to do versus what you think you should do, and more.

PART 5 REACHING RECONCILIATION

Enneagram Type Four

Head Center Opening

- [ ] Develop insights of the mind in addition to insights of the heart. Ask yourself this question first: *What do I think is true?* Then ask, *What do I feel is true?*

- [ ] Examine your specific thoughts but also how you think – meta-level thinking; this approach opens up more complete access to your Head Center.

Heart Center Opening

- [ ] Examine your perceptions about what other people are feeling regarding you, outside events, and issues in general; make sure you are not projecting your own fears and emotional reactions onto others.

- [ ] Remember that intensity in any form does not create balance and wholeness; intense emotionality is no exception. Aspire to be more emotionally balanced.

Body Center Opening

- [ ] Don't let feelings immobilize you and prevent you from doing anything; action is one way to move through emotional reactions. Experiment with this.

- [ ] Ask yourself on a regular basis about your somatic reactions to these questions: *What do I really want? What should I do here?* Listen to your somatic responses. Pay as much attention to your somatic reactions as you do to your emotional responses.

PART 5 REACHING RECONCILIATION

Enneagram Type Five **5**

Head Center Opening

- [ ] Remember that logical analysis is not necessarily objective; logic can have its own bias, depending on the logic used. Challenge your own thinking and reflect on how much you rely on logic instead of your emotional and somatic responses.

- [ ] Consider that feelings are actually sources of information just as much as facts. Make sure your insights also include information about feelings and somatic responses.

Heart Center Opening

- [ ] Learn to feel your own emotions in real time, not after the fact. This will enable you to know yourself better, to read other people's feelings more accurately, and to develop more empathy.

- [ ] Create fewer communication barriers between yourself and other people. Gradually share more information about yourself with others. Ask people questions about themselves. This is not intrusive; it shows interest in them.

Body Center Opening

- [ ] Learn to read your body's signals so that you can trust your physical reactions. Breathing into your body – and not just breathing into your head – will open your somatic access.

- [ ] Develop more of your tactile sense by touching different items and textures more often and exploring what you experience when you do so. It can be fabric, a countertop, hair, food, a pet. The sense of touch allows us greater connectedness to the world outside us.

PART 5 REACHING RECONCILIATION

Enneagram Type Six

Head Center Opening

☐ Slow down your thirst for and analysis of data, particularly when you are anxious or notice that you are repeating the same thoughts. Explore what drives you to want information so badly.

☐ Learn to differentiate your projections from objective insights by honestly examining your own feelings and motivations. This will help you clarify your thoughts and project with less intensity or less often.

Heart Center Opening

☐ Remain empathic even when someone's behavior bothers, hurts, or angers you. Allow your heart to be touched without over-relying on your thoughts or Head Center.

☐ Be true to yourself even when you need or want something from another person; refrain from engaging in ingratiating behavior when you feel afraid.

Body Center Opening

☐ Take deliberative, considered, thoughtful action that is also timely: not too fast and not too slow. Go "ready, aim, fire," not "ready, ready, aim, aim, fire" and not "aim, fire, fire, fire."

☐ When you are unsure of what to do or you find your mind stirring and rehashing old information, engage in physical activity: walking, biking, stretching, dancing. As you do this, ask your body for its somatic wisdom.

PART 5 REACHING RECONCILIATION

Enneagram Type Seven

Head Center Opening

- [ ] To have insight takes time and reflection; allow yourself both more time and more self-reflection in order to get a deeper perspective.
- [ ] Do you get intoxicated by new ideas, whether they come from you or someone else? Learn to focus your mind on one idea at a time.

Heart Center Opening

- [ ] Explore your feelings; be curious about them; learn to read the internal cues to your emotional states.
- [ ] Consider the potential impact on people of everything you think, feel and do. Breathe into your heart as you do this.

Body Center Opening

- [ ] Slow your pace and relax your breathing, making sure you inhale and allow the air to move throughout your body. Inhabit your whole body, using your breath as a guide.
- [ ] Bypass your tendency to over-think and over-plan by developing your instinctual or body-based knowing. When considering options, ask yourself: *Which of these options does my body - not my mind - tell me will lead to the best outcome?*

PART 5 REACHING RECONCILIATION

Enneagram Type Eight 8

Head Center Opening

- [ ] Question your assumptions; ask the opinions of others; take in multiple viewpoints.
- [ ] Maintain your ability to do big-picture planning, but make sure you also plan for the operational aspects of implementation. Details do matter.

Heart Center Opening

- [ ] Take the time to sense the feelings of other people, even when you don't respect the individuals.
- [ ] Become more aware of your tendency to present yourself as bold and confident; when you allow yourself to be more vulnerable, people will support you more.

Body Center Opening

- [ ] Before you take action, especially quick immediate action, pause and reflect on why you are doing so.
- [ ] You can trust your somatic responses in many cases. However, when your reaction is very strong or quick, pause and re-examine what you are about to do.

PART 5 REACHING RECONCILIATION

Enneagram Type Nine

Head Center Opening

☐ Remember that when you gather too much information and either overanalyze a situation or perceive it from too many points of view, this creates confusion for you and others.

☐ Keep to your deadlines by planning your time schedule carefully and then following through.

Heart Center Opening

☐ Make sure to maintain your empathy, even with people you perceive as negative and complaining.

☐ Maintain an attitude of kindness even toward people who stridently disagree with you.

Body Center Opening

☐ Figure out why you procrastinate; err on the side of taking action too quickly rather than too slowly.

☐ Without being stubborn, hold firm on decisions and opinions that you believe are best, even in the face of opposition and conflict.

PART 5 REACHING RECONCILIATION

INTEGRATING YOUR CENTERS THROUGH MUSIC

Music is a wonderful way to first access and then integrate your Centers. To use music in this, two things must be considered: (1) choosing the music that resonates with each Center, and (2) your being able to experience music somatically. Not everyone feels music in their body, but this music works for those who do.

Head Center music
Most classical music and most jazz

Heart Center music
Most country western

Body Center music
Most Motown, drumming music

All three Centers
Bolero by Ravel

To use music to open your Centers of Intelligence, find a place where you can listen to a good recording. If possible, close your eyes while listening and feel the music inside your body where it most resonates within you. The suggested Head Center music will most likely vibrate in your Head Center and so on for each Center.

Bolero, which is a longer musical piece, vibrates first in the Head Center, then in the Heart Center, and then in the Body Center.

You can do this sitting down, lying down, or moving to the music in space. All of these ways work as long as you can feel the musical vibrations in your body.

Reflect on your experiences with music as a way to integrate the Centers.

PART 5 REACHING RECONCILIATION

ARROWS

Your arrows, the two types that point toward and away from your core Enneagram type, can be used for psychological as well as spiritual development. For psychological development, each arrow contains some qualities or attributes that can help you be more resourced, flexible, and versatile. This can help loosen or lessen your type-based reactivity.

For spiritual development, using the arrows can be profound. They are energy flows and dynamic currents rather than holders of specific qualities. They are perspectives and energetic forces that form a triangle with our core type. And any of the types in the triangle – core type and two arrows – can function as any of the three forces of affirming, denying and reconciling.

To use the triangular configuration for spiritual and transformative development, it is best to start with the energy and perspective of your own type (the 1st or affirming force), then move to one of your other arrows as the denying or 2nd force, and then to the remaining arrow as the reconciling force.

ASK THE MAP

You can use an Enneagram symbol floor map for this because it helps fully embody the energies of the types, not just their qualities. In addition, moving deliberately, consciously, and slowly along the arrow lines helps you do several things:

Sense the energy inherent in the arrow line.

Ask a focused question as you walk along the line so you get an answer from the energy of the line itself.

Allow the time to relax and even surrender to the energy and wisdom of the arrow line as you walk.

Step One: Start on your type number

First, stand on your Enneagram type number, feel the map under your feet and through your legs and torso. Instead of asking the map a specific question, verbalize an issue or a strong reaction you are having to something. Breathe and stay relaxed. Allow a response from your type to emerge and feel the energy underlying this response. Your type, in this context, might be the 1st force, the affirming energy. Or it might be the 2nd force, the denying energy. Which is it?

PART 5 REACHING RECONCILIATION

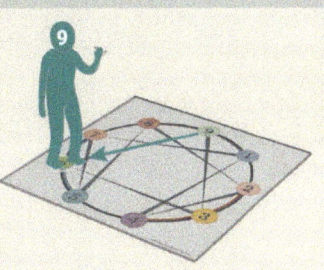

Step 2: Walk arrow line

Second, consider your arrow lines. Which arrow line or type at the end of this arrow line might be the opposing force to your type's energy?

Walk slowly along that arrow line while you ask this: *What deeper truth is revealed about this issue as I walk this arrow?* Once you arrive at the type number of the arrow, slowly turn toward the middle of the symbol, breathe, and ask this: *What is your perspective on this issue, one that is contrary to my type-based response?* This is the 2nd force, the denying energy, if your core type is the affirming force in this situation. If your core type is the denying force, then this arrow line is the affirming force.

Step 3: Walk back to your core type

Step 4: Walk the second arrow line

Fourth, as you remain embodied, walk slowly along the arrow line to the arrow's type. Once you arrive at the type number of the arrow, slowly turn toward the middle of the symbol and breathe gently and fully. Then ask this: *What is your perspective on this issue, one that embraces and reconciles what's already been revealed?* Allow the answer to emerge; experience the energy of this somatically. This is the 3rd force, the reconciling energy.

Step 5: Return to your core type

Finally, return to your Enneagram type number, walking along the same arrow as in step 4, and stand on your type number. What do you experience there, mentally, emotionally, and somatically? What wisdom emerges?

PART 5 REACHING RECONCILIATION

HARMONIC TRIADS

The types with these three triads - optimistic, competency and intensity - have strong similarities and some similar challenges. Once you know your type and the triad to which you belong, the triad-based challenges bring increased awareness and the common growth areas and practices offer transformational opportunities.

These triads, sometimes called the harmonic triads, include the optimistic triad, sometimes called the "positive outlook" triad, the competency triad, and the intensity triad, sometimes referred to as the "reactive" triad.

OPTIMISTIC TRIAD: TYPES 2 – 7 – 9

Triad Strategy Maintain a positive emotional environment, both internal and external, while minimizing pain, discomfort, or conflict

2s perceive positive motivations or intentions to see the best in and reinforce connections with others.

7s reframe difficulties to preserve positivity.

9s diffuse their focus or 'numb out' to negative aspects of reality to maintain harmony.

Challenges for the optimistic triad

Avoidance, glossing over and/or minimizing painful truths about self, others and/or situations

Risk of spiritual or emotional bypassing

Growth for the optimistic triad

Invite the full emotional range of feelings, in addition to joy and happiness, such as grief, sorrow, frustration, anger and fear.

Stay with uncomfortable feelings and discomfort without needing to fix or transcend them, in yourself, in others or in relationships.

PART 5 REACHING RECONCILIATION

PRACTICES FOR THE OPTIMISTIC TRIAD

Both Sides Instead of searching for and finding the upside of what occurs, also focus your attention on the downside. Answer these questions:

What's hard right now?

How do I make it okay to feel the emotions that arise and to stay with them?

What if my continuous positive intentions are actually keeping me from being more introspective and truthful with myself?

Going Deep Go deeper, beyond your initial response. Answer these questions:

What am I actually feeling beneath my smile?

Do I have many different smiles, each one with a different meaning? What are they?

PART 5 REACHING RECONCILIATION

PRACTICES FOR THE OPTIMISTIC TRIAD (CONTINUED)

Being Present Being present to others means you first have to be present to yourself. Sit quietly for 10 minutes with a challenging feeling or experience. Do not distract yourself in any way. Before you do this activity, answer the questions below. After that, do the activity, sit with your experience, and allow what emerges.

Do I think I can do this?

What would make it easier for me to do?

What would make it harder?

How does my Enneagram type factor into my willingness or ability to do this?

PART 5 REACHING RECONCILIATION

COMPETENCY TRIAD: TYPES 1 – 3 – 5

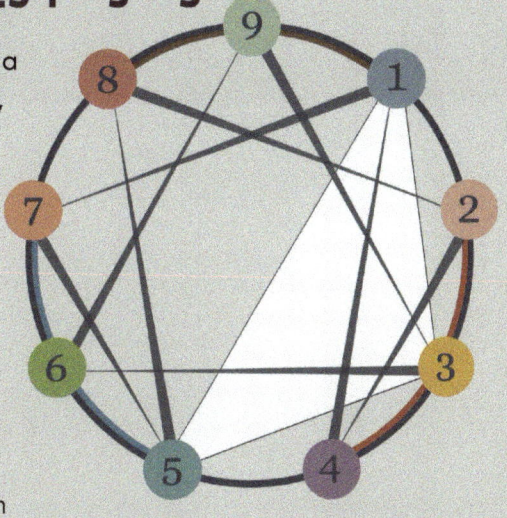

Triad Strategy Engage almost everything as a problem to be solved with logic, objectivity, effectiveness and rationality; work with feelings as issues that need to be minimized and resolved in a systematic, efficient way

1s define competency as being right or correct, in both opinions and actions.

3s define competency as knowing how to get results.

5s define competency as having a thorough and fact-based knowledge base.

Challenges for the competency triad

Over-emphasize and over-value tasks and performance, control, and different forms of emotional disengagement, and undervalue vulnerability and receptivity

Risk appearing cold, unfeeling, overly independent, and controlling

Growth for the competency triad

Access and integrate emotional and relational intelligence with your focus on tasks and performance.

Allow yourself to be seen, felt and supported without your needing to feel and be perceived as competent.

Intentionality Intentionally try something you're not good at. After you do, answer these questions:

How did I feel doing something I think I'm not good at?

What did I learn about myself?

PART 5 REACHING RECONCILIATION

PRACTICES FOR THE COMPETENCY TRIAD (CONTINUED)

Once you've answered the previous questions, try something you don't know whether or not you'll be good at. Answer these questions:

How did I feel doing something I didn't know in advance whether I'd be good at or not?

What did I learn about myself from this?

Express Yourself Share one thing you're proud of with someone and one thing you're struggling with. Offer no explanations to that person, just keep it real. After you do, answer these questions:

What was more challenging to share, the thing I'm proud of or the issue I struggle with?

How might the answer above be connected to my Enneagram type, the content of what I share, or the person I chose?

How do I feel now for having done something out of my comfort zone, such as sharing my feelings?

What would help me do this more often?

PART 5 REACHING RECONCILIATION

Ask for Help Choose something small at first. Select someone and ask them for support in some way. The important part is for you to notice how you respond mentally, emotionally, and somatically when you ask and get their response. Once you do this, answer the following questions:

Who did I select and why?

What did I choose to ask for help about and why?

How did I experience asking for help?

How is my reaction related to my Enneagram type?

For my own growth, how can I best take this process forward?

PART 5 REACHING RECONCILIATION

PRACTICES FOR THE COMPETENCY TRIAD (CONTINUED)

Feel Don't Fix In stressful moments or moments of uncertainty, pause before you take action. Ask yourself this: *What am I feeling right now and needing to reflect on before I take action?* After you have practiced this way of pausing at least three times, answer these questions:

Under stress and uncertainty, do I tend to act fast or retract and not act very quickly?

How is my reaction above related to my Enneagram type?

What lies underneath my tendency to take quick action and fix things?

INTENSITY TRIAD: TYPES 4 – 6 – 8

Triad Strategy Express themselves directly, honestly, and intensely, especially when feeling disappointed, anxious or mistrusting, while also seeking truthful responses from others

4s exhibit emotional intensity.

6s exhibit mental intensity.

8s exhibit somatic intensity.

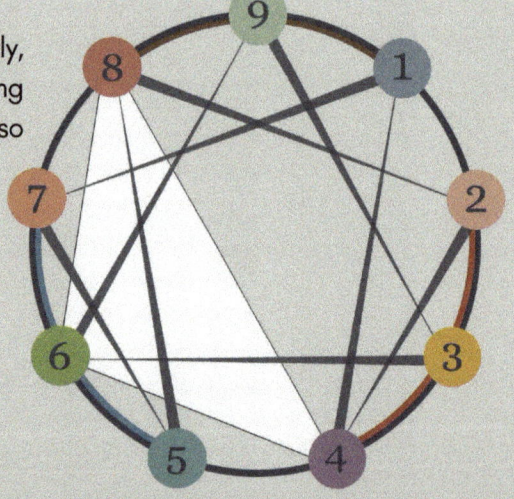

PART 5 REACHING RECONCILIATION

Challenges for the intensity triad

May react instantaneously out of reactivity instead of grounded clarity

Risk driving others away through their high intensity or hypervigilant approach

Growth for the intensity triad

Learn to self-regulate intensity spikes without suppressing them.

Explore what lies beneath your high or fluctuating intensity levels by cultivating inner balance.

PRACTICES FOR THE INTENSITY TRIAD

Breathe Before you react, take three deep breaths. Instead of reacting, give yourself time to reflect by asking yourself this: *What is the real need or the real feeling or fear beneath the rise in my intensity?*

Safety Reset Identify what makes you feel emotionally safe. Make that list here:

Safety factor 1

Safety factor 2

Safety factor 3

Are these factors within your control or outside?

If you could actually control these factors, would you be satisfied and truly feel safe?

PART 5 REACHING RECONCILIATION

PRACTICES FOR THE INTENSITY TRIAD (CONTINUED)

As you reflect on your list and answers about safety, what are your thoughts and feelings now about your intensity and its causes from the prior page?

Watch the Movie Practice observing your thoughts, emotions and desire rather than reacting so quickly. By observing yourself first, it's as if you're observing your own movie. As you think about your movie in the past, how would you describe it in terms of storyline, tone, intensity, and more?

Be More Vulnerable in Your Truth-Telling Instead of escalating your intensity when communicating with someone about something important to you, say this instead: *Here's what's really going on within me, and here is what I hope for as an outcome of this conversation.*

After you do this, write down how this went, how you felt or experienced it, what you might want to repeat, and what you might do differently.

PART 5 REACHING RECONCILIATION

INVISIBLE TRIANGLES

These groupings of three types are not the same as the earlier triads and are based on what is called object relations that influence how we relate to others in our world. The three groupings include the attachment trio (3-6-9), the frustration trio (1-4-7), and the rejection trio (2-5-8). Enneagram types in these groupings share similarities in terms of relationships with others, and their shared development areas can be profound and transformative.

These are referred to as the invisible triangle groupings because the Enneagram was originally comprised of three triangles, but the lines going between numbers 4 and 7 and between numbers 2 and 5 are no longer visible.

3-6-9: ATTACHMENT TRIO

Deep Concern: Not being truly seen; losing connection to self, others, spiritual world

Primary Strategy: Seek security by attaching to roles, routines, or relationships

Secondary Strategy: Over-adapt, become mute or mold authentic self to maintain harmony in relationships

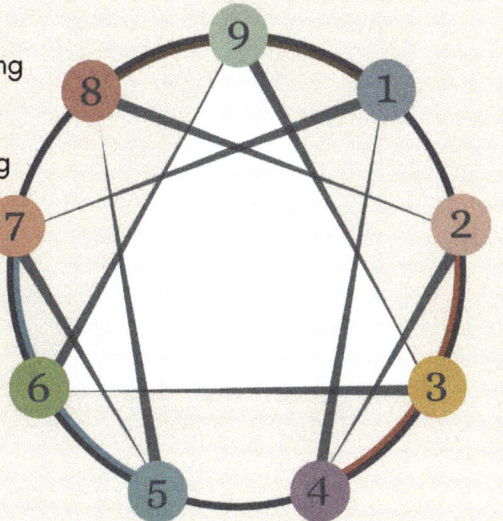

Challenges for the attachment trio

Difficulty tolerating disapproval or instability

Over-identification with something outside themselves such as people, roles or routines

Growth for the attachment trio

Be willing to disappoint others for the sake of their own integrity.

Stay present when structures dissolve and have trust that clarity will then emerge.

PART 5 REACHING RECONCILIATION

PRACTICES FOR THE ATTACHMENT TRIO

Interrupt Automatic Adaptation Notice when you're overly adjusting to others or systems and stop.

What will it take for you to stop?

Name Your Core Need Ask yourself this question on a regular basis: *What am I trying to hold onto, keep constant, or stabilize?*

If you had to answer that question right now, what would your answer be?

Reclaim Your Inner Authority Practice making decisions from internal clarity instead of basing your decisions on something external such as an authority figure, someone with whom you are close, or a role model. You'll need to address this issue each time you make a decision and are about to act.

What is your heart's desire?

PART 5 REACHING RECONCILIATION

1-4-7: FRUSTRATION TRIO

Deep Concern: The world not matching their internal ideals; deep disappointment

Primary Strategy: Focus on what's missing, not right or what they can't get

Secondary Strategy: Chase aspirations, ideals and possibilities; crave idealized states

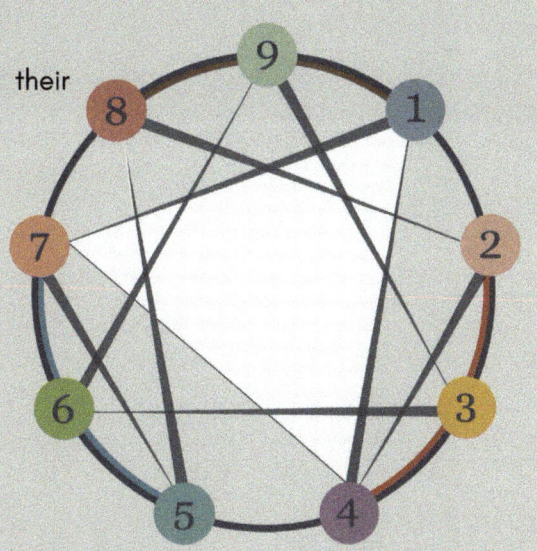

Challenges for the frustration trio

Chronic dissatisfaction or restlessness

Resistance to how things are and to ordinary experiences

Growth for the frustration trio

Find depth and meaning in what's already here, not that which isn't.

Experiment with enjoyment and gratitude without changing or improving anything.

PRACTICES FOR THE FRUSTRATION TRIO

Welcome Imperfection Engage with the "good enough" aspects of yourself and others. Look internally and externally. What do you notice right now that is "good enough" in both you and others?

What is "good enough" now in my life: in me, others, and my situation?

PART 5 REACHING RECONCILIATION

PRACTICES FOR THE FRUSTRATION TRIO (CONTINUED)

Soften Expectations Notice how your idealism can block satisfaction or spontaneity.

Would you rather keep your idealism and block your satisfaction and spontaneity or increase your satisfaction and spontaneity by relaxing the intensity of your idealism?

Stay in the Present Moment Notice and appreciate what is, not just what could or should be. To help you do this, stay more in the present moment. There's power in the NOW. Write down all of the things you are aware of right now.

PART 5 REACHING RECONCILIATION

2-5-8: REJECTION TRIO

Deep Concern: Being rejected for who they are, their needs and their vulnerability

Primary Strategy: Reject or create distance from others first before they get rejected

Secondary Strategy: Control the terms of connection and distance

Challenges for the rejection trio

Aversion to emotional exposure and vulnerability

Loss of control of relational dynamics

Growth for the rejection trio

Let someone see what you hide.

Practice connection as mutual and reciprocal, not transactional or protective.

PRACTICES FOR THE REJECTION TRIO

Allow Vulnerability Breathe into the parts of you, especially your body, that control your expressions of vulnerability.

What parts of your body hold or control your emotional expression and vulnerability?

Push Pause Take a moment to pause before taking charge, moving toward someone or withdrawing. Consider what you are feeling, and explore your choices or options.

Do you tend to take charge (like an 8), move toward (like a 2) or withdraw (like a 5)?

PART 5 REACHING RECONCILIATION

PRACTICES FOR THE REJECTION TRIO (CONTINUED)

Relinquish the Stance of "Not Needing" Experiment with expressing needs, not just offering strength, resources, or acting like you don't need anything.

List your needs here and who might meet them.

INSTINCTS

The three basic instincts highlight the ways we try to get our needs met: self-preservation, social, and one-to-one (also called sexual or intimacy). This doesn't mean that our needs are actually getting satisfied in these three instinctual arenas; it's just that we try! Here is what the three instincts mean.

Self-preservation safety, security, danger, resources, structure, and control
Social belonging, community, groups, social relationships, and influence
One-to-one intimacy, affection, relations with one other person, bonding, and attraction

The question is simple: *What do you need in each instinctual arena?* The answer to this question is more complex.

PART 5 REACHING RECONCILIATION

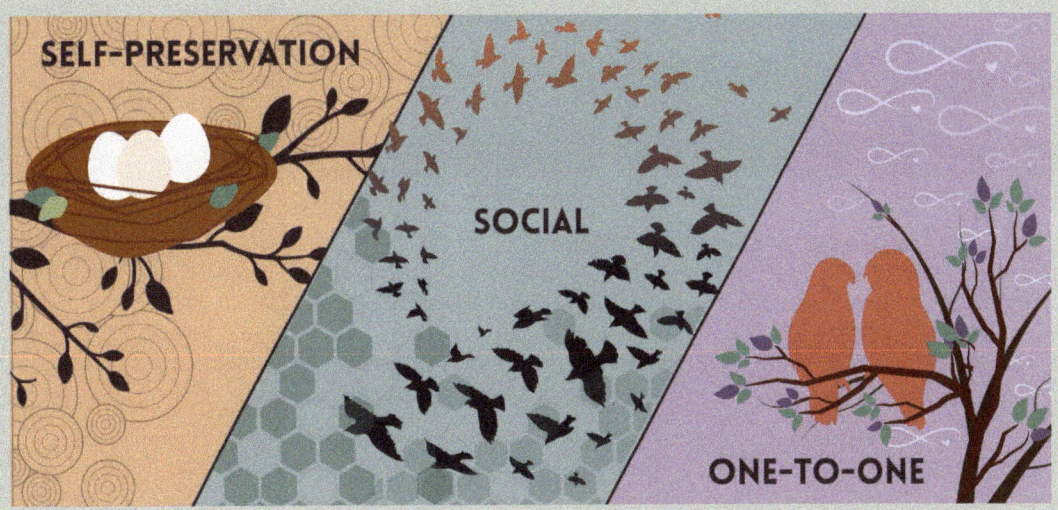

INSTINCTS: TRUE NEEDS VERSUS FALSE NEEDS

When we respond to this question – what do you need in each instinctual area – the answer we give is primarily coming from our type-based ego structure. It's nearly impossible to answer any other way given that our "normal" responses arise from our ego structure. Of course, the intensity of these responses can vary depending on our level of self-mastery and psychological and spiritual development.

There is a path toward transformation using instincts if you inquire what you need in each arena, but ask the questions and get a response from the higher state of your Heart Center of Intelligence. This is known as the Virtue of your type.

The question is the same: *What do you need in each instinctual arena?* The answer, because it comes from the higher state, is enlightening.

FREEING THE INSTINCTS FROM THE HIGHER EMOTIONAL STATE

To free your instincts – in other words, disentangle the Passion or emotional habit of your type from the instincts – you need to get yourself in the higher state of your Heart Center, known as the Virtue. The following information describes the Passion to Virtue transformation for each type, followed by a type-specific activity that helps you re-experience the higher emotional state for your Enneagram type. Once you can stay in this higher state, then answer the three questions about your instinctual needs.

What do you need in the self-preservation arena?

What do you need in the social arena?

What do you need in the one-to-one arena?

PART 5 REACHING RECONCILIATION

FREEING THE INSTINCTS

Enneagram Type One

From anger (passion) to serenity (virtue)

Serenity: an open-hearted acceptance of all that occurs

Remember a time when you experienced a sense of deep calmness and complete acceptance no matter how angry you felt or what was occurring within you. Stay with that memory, reliving and embodying what was occurring within you at that moment of serenity.

As you stay in this higher emotional state, ask and answer these three questions:

What do you need in the self-preservation arena?

What do you need in the social arena?

What do you need in the one-to-one arena?

PART 5 REACHING RECONCILIATION

FREEING THE INSTINCTS

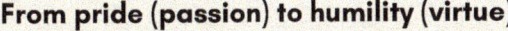
Enneagram Type Two

From pride (passion) to humility (virtue)

Humility: feelings of complete self-acceptance and self-worth without either self-inflation or self-deflation based on the opinions of others

Remember a time when you were able to maintain a sincere, modest and realistic sense of self-worth, even when something went very well or didn't go as you had wanted, so you did not inflate or deflate your self-esteem (based on the reactions of others). Stay with that memory, re-living and embodying what was occurring within you at that moment of humility.

As you stay in this higher emotional state, ask and answer these three questions:

What do you need in the self-preservation arena?

What do you need in the social arena?

What do you need in the one-to-one arena?

PART 5 REACHING RECONCILIATION

FREEING THE INSTINCTS

Enneagram Type Three

From deceit (passion) to truthfulness (virtue)

Truthfulness: finding true self-acceptance through acknowledging both your successes and failures, realizing your image is not your essence

Remember a time when, instead of not telling the complete truth to yourself or someone else, you told the truth about yourself and your situation and completely accepted yourself as you are. Stay with that memory, reliving and embodying what was occurring within you at that moment of truthfulness.

As you stay in this higher emotional state, ask and answer these three questions:

What do you need in the self-preservation arena?

What do you need in the social arena?

What do you need in the one-to-one arena?

PART 5 REACHING RECONCILIATION

FREEING THE INSTINCTS

Enneagram Type Four

From envy (passion) to balance (virtue)

Balance: experiencing your inner emotional state in such a clear and centered way that thought, feeling and action emanate from your steady and integrated inner self

Remember a time when you didn't compare yourself to anyone and felt at peace with who you are and what you have to offer. Stay with that memory, reliving and embodying what was occurring within you at that moment of emotional balance.

As you stay in this higher emotional state, ask and answer these three questions:

What do you need in the self-preservation arena?

What do you need in the social arena?

What do you need in the one-to-one arena?

PART 5 REACHING RECONCILIATION

FREEING THE INSTINCTS

Enneagram Type Five — 5

From avarice (passion) to non-attachment (virtue)

Non-attachment: the first-hand understanding that detachment from feelings, people and experience is not non-attachment and that you must first fully engage and care about something before you can then become non-attached

Remember a time when you were fully sharing, forthcoming and present with others and while you cared deeply about them and the situation, you were also able to let go and to be totally free from your own attachment. Stay with that memory, reliving and embodying what was occurring within you at that moment of non-attachment.

As you stay in this higher emotional state, ask and answer these three questions:

What do you need in the self-preservation arena?

What do you need in the social arena?

What do you need in the one-to-one arena?

PART 5 REACHING RECONCILIATION

FREEING THE INSTINCTS

Enneagram Type Six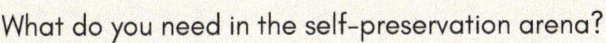

From fear (passion) to courage (virtue)

Courage: the feeling of being fully capable of overcoming fear through clear and fully conscious action, rather than turning to either inaction or action designed to prove you have no fear

Remember a time when you were courageous and able to overcome your fears in a fully conscious and calm way. Stay with that memory, reliving and embodying what was occurring within you at that moment of courage.

As you stay in this higher emotional state, ask and answer these three questions:

What do you need in the self-preservation arena?

What do you need in the social arena?

What do you need in the one-to-one arena?

PART 5 REACHING RECONCILIATION

FREEING THE INSTINCTS

Enneagram Type Seven

From gluttony (passion) to sobriety (virtue)

Sobriety: feeling full, complete, satisfied and whole, which comes from pursuing, staying with, and integrating painful and difficult experiences as well as pleasurable and stimulating ones

Remember a time when you felt integrated and complete as a person because you were able to absorb both the difficult and the pleasurable aspects of a situation. Stay with that memory, reliving and embodying what was occurring within you at that moment of sobriety.

As you stay in this higher emotional state, ask and answer these three questions:

What do you need in the self-preservation arena?

What do you need in the social arena?

What do you need in the one-to-one arena?

PART 5 REACHING RECONCILIATION

FREEING THE INSTINCTS

Enneagram Type Eight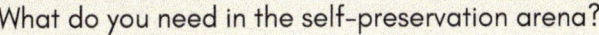

From lust (passion) to innocence (virtue)

Innocence: the childlike feeling of vulnerability and openness, such that the need to control situations or protect yourself and others is no longer present

Remember a time when you felt the pure innocent openness of a child without needing to control the situation or protect yourself and others. Stay with that memory, reliving and embodying what was occurring within you at that moment of innocence.

As you stay in this higher emotional state, ask and answer these three questions:

What do you need in the self-preservation arena?

What do you need in the social arena?

What do you need in the one-to-one arena?

PART 5 REACHING RECONCILIATION

FREEING THE INSTINCTS

Enneagram Type Nine

From laziness (passion) to right action (virtue)

Right action: being so fully present to yourself and others that you know exactly what you feel and what action to take

Remember a time when you felt totally present and aware of yourself and others, so you knew instinctively how you felt and what you must do. Stay with that memory, reliving and embodying what was occurring within you at that moment of right action.

As you stay in this higher emotional state, ask and answer these three questions:

What do you need in the self-preservation arena?

What do you need in the social arena?

What do you need in the one-to-one arena?

PART 5 REACHING RECONCILIATION

INSTINCTS AND THE LAW OF THREE

Wholeness, integration and transformation include balancing and utilizing all three instincts in accordance with the Law of Three. Any of the instincts can serve as any of the three forces: affirming, denying or reconciling, although they most often function in this way:

Most common force for each instinct

One-to-One instinct: Affirming 1st force by initiating with energy, drive, intensity magnetism, and forward momentum

Self-preserving instinct: Denying 2nd force by pushing back with caution, concerns, protection, and safety

Social instinct: Reconciling 3rd force by bridging, integrating, linking to a larger whole or perspective

RECONCILING — THIRD FORCE — INTEGRATES AND TRANSFORMS — **SOCIAL**

PUSHES BACK

INITIATES CHANGE

DENYING — SECOND FORCE — **SELF-PRESERVING**

AFFIRMING — FIRST FORCE — **ONE-TO-ONE**

Context, however, matters. In a famine, the self-preservation instinct may become the affirming force in order to get food for yourself; the social instinct becomes the denying force – you can't get food or take it from other people, for example; and the one-to-one instinct may become the reconciling force where you fuse/bond with another person to gather food for survival.

What's important for wholeness is (1) being able to access, use, and honor all three instincts, not just one or two, (2) to do so in the context of the Law of Three, and (3) to have instinctual flexibility so that any of the instincts can function as any of the forces, when needed.

PART 5 REACHING RECONCILIATION

INSTINCTS AND THE LAW OF THREE (CONTINUED)

What's an example of how the Law of Three and the three instincts have manifested in your life?

Can you think of an example in your life where the instincts played different forces from the example above? What was it?

If you can't think of one, take the example from the first question and think about what would have happened if your instincts had been used in a different way, as a different force. What would have happened then?

PART 5 REACHING RECONCILIATION

SUBTYPES

Enneagram subtypes are three sub-versions of each type, with all three subtypes sharing the same thinking and feeling patterns, as well as ego ideals and primary defense mechanisms. The subtypes of each type can differ from one another in some of their behavior and the situations that activate their reactivity.

Our subtype is formed through the dynamic interaction between our Enneagram type passion – repeating emotional response pattern – and one of our instincts: self-preservation, social or one-to-one. Once this occurs, the instinct then becomes distorted by the passion. This combination of type-based passion and instinct creates three versions of each type.

We can have more than one active subtype. They may function so that one subtype is far more active than the other, or two subtypes can be equally active. It is also possible that one subtype may be more active at certain times in our life or under different circumstances.

It is worth noting that once our Enneagram type-based subtype is particularly triggered, it is very challenging to push pause because our subtype-based response happens so quickly. At the same time, this intense subtype reactivity also makes it a potential catalyst for enormous growth and even transformation.

There are many ways to use subtypes for growth; here are three possibilities:

Subtype-based awareness of triggers – promotes comfort
Just being aware of our subtype and the triggers for our subtype reactivity are enough to get our attention over time and to help us relax our responses.

Specific subtype development activities – promotes progress
Specific development activities for each subtype of a type are especially useful.

Catalytic conversions through subtypes – promotes breakthroughs
When we are in the throes of our subtype-based reactivity, it is an intense experience. However, if we can allow a pause instead of a reaction and sit in the energy of our reactivity, it can create profound changes within us. (The catalytic conversion process is described at the end of the subtype triggers and development activities on page 199.)

What kind of change are you seeking? Comfort (via awareness)? Progress (via subtype-based development activities) or breakthroughs (via catalytic conversions)?

PART 5 REACHING RECONCILIATION

SUBTYPE-BASED DEVELOPMENT

Here is information about the passion or emotional habit of each type, the name for and a description of each subtype, reactivity triggers for that subtype, and what to notice in yourself and an activity to increase your self-awareness. This is followed by a specific development idea that is particularly useful for people of that subtype.

If you know your type-based subtype, you can go to that information below and ask yourself if you are willing to engage in the suggested activities to reduce your subtype reactivity. Remember you may have more than one active subtype, so you can feel free to use multiple activities.

Enneagram Type One

Emotional passion of ANGER The chronic dissatisfaction with self, others, life and work that are not as they should be

Self-Preservation One subtypes ("worry") focus on getting everything structured, controlled, precise, and organized correctly, and experience anxiety, worry, and irritation when they think this may not happen.

Self-Preservation One subtype trigger: Not being told how or not knowing how to structure something so that no mistakes occur.

Awareness activity: Notice the true or deeper sources of your anger, anxiety and thoughts about imperfection and control; relax more.

Development activity: Breathe fully and in a relaxing way, then tell yourself this: *There's no need to worry. You can stop worrying now. You've got this!*

Social One subtypes ("non-adaptability") perceive themselves as role models of the right way of behaving and believe they set the standard for how others should be; they lead and influence by example, focusing their efforts on critiquing social institutions as a way to perfect them.

Social One subtype trigger: Not being treated as if they are the best role model.

Awareness activity: Notice your need to be right and perfect in the world; learn that your worth doesn't depend on your being a near-perfect role model.

Development activity: Answer these questions in depth: *Who actually asked me to be a role model for them? What is the price I pay for trying to be a near-perfect role model in terms of my relationships with others?*

PART 5 REACHING RECONCILIATION

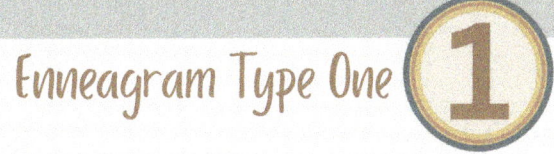

Enneagram Type One

One-to-One One subtypes ("zeal") have intense need to perfect others, particularly those who matter to them and to perfect society in general, perceive critiquing and reforming others as both their right and responsibility.

One-to-One One subtype trigger: Others, especially those who you are trying to perfect, do not meet your expectations or respond negatively to your criticisms.

Awareness activity: Notice your need to improve and reform others; focus less on critiquing others and more on your own self-acceptance.

Development activity: Notice your intense forward energy when you are about to make a comment to someone they might feel is critical. At that moment, bring your energy back into yourself instead of saying something. Take a relaxed breath, breathing into your heart area, and ask yourself: *What am feeling right now about myself? Is there something about me I need to be more accepting of?*

As a One, what do I think is my primary subtype?

Am I willing to engage in the recommended development activity for my subtype?

What would help and hinder me in doing this?

PART 5 REACHING RECONCILIATION

SUBTYPE-BASED DEVELOPMENT

Enneagram Type Two

Emotional passion of PRIDE Having your self-worth and importance integrally linked with how others respond, feeling inflated when there is a positive response and feeling deflated with a negative reaction

Self-Preservation Two subtypes ("me-first/privilege") deny their own needs for protection, try to attract others to protect them by both being appealing and appearing to be innocent and blameless, even childlike; they can be ambivalent about closeness and trusting others.

Self-Preservation Two subtype trigger: Not being acknowledged or catered to in ways you want or expect from others.

Awareness activity: Notice how your fear and ambivalence in relationships hurt intimacy; develop more resilience, personal power, and capacity for intimacy.

Development activity: Make a list of the ways you keep yourself small, younger than you are, more childlike. Once you do this, write down what you actually gain from doing this. Then make a list of the ways in which this behavior causes problems for you or no longer serves you. Reflect on these lists in terms of what you really want from your life right now.

Social Two subtypes ("ambition") focus on helping groups more than individuals, are more intellectually oriented and more comfortable being in visibly powerful positions than other Twos, which is a result of their desire to stand above the group but without appearing they are doing so.

Social Two subtype trigger: Feeling disappointed in or marginalized by a social group in which you have wielded leadership or influence.

Awareness activity: Notice how your need for power and admiration has a strategic intent that hinders closeness with others; focus on your own feelings and needs.

Development activity: When you are thinking about taking a central role or making a commitment to a group that will demand a great deal of your time and energy, ask yourself why you are really thinking about doing this. Don't settle for an answer that describes your commitment to a cause or a group purpose. Instead, ask yourself about your deeper, more personal motivations.

PART 5 REACHING RECONCILIATION

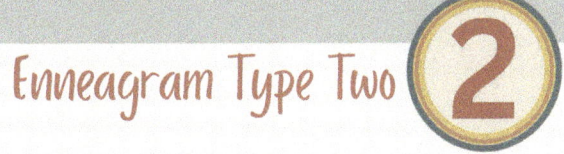

Enneagram Type Two

One-to-One Two subtypes ("aggression/seduction") are oriented to individual relationships and meeting the needs of important people and partners, attracting these others as a way to both feel important and hoping and expecting that these individuals will satisfy their needs in exchange.

One-to-One Two subtype trigger: Feeling threatened by someone coming between you and a person with whom you want or already have a special relationship.

Awareness activity: Notice how you pursue intense and energetic relations with others in order to get them to meet your needs; find ways of satisfying your own needs.

Development activity: Strive for more reciprocity in your relationships so that you are not the only or primary one giving in the relationship. You also have to be willing to ask others for what you need more directly so they know you actually need something from them. If they are not interested in reciprocation, ask yourself if you really want to be involved in non-reciprocal relationships.

As a Two, what do I think is my primary subtype?

Am I willing to engage in the recommended activity for my subtype?

What would help and hinder me in doing this?

PART 5 REACHING RECONCILIATION

SUBTYPE-BASED DEVELOPMENT

Enneagram Type Three

Emotional passion of DECEIT Needing to appear successful to gain the admiration and respect of others, avoiding failure by hiding parts of yourself and believing that your image is your true self

Self-Preservation Three subtypes ("security") want to be seen as a good or ideal person who is self-reliant, autonomous, hardworking; they have an image of having no image and of being authentic.

Self-Preservation Three subtype trigger: Having your image of no image (your authenticity) challenged directly or indirectly.

Awareness activity: Notice how you move fast, like to create structure as a way to feel more certain or secure, and allow yourself little time for your feelings and desires to emerge; find a deeper connection with yourself and others.

Development activity: Notice how your shoulders become extremely tense and rise when you feel stressed or are driving yourself to get things done. When this occurs, stop, relax your shoulders by taking deep breaths, and stay in this less tense state for at least two minutes. Proceed with what you were doing, but without the push and tension.

Social Three subtypes ("prestige") want to be seen as successful and admirable in the context of specific social groups and like being around other successful people because they believe this proximity reinforces their own positive image and status.

Social Three subtype trigger: Feeling unable to gain acceptance from high-status social groups to which you want to belong.

Awareness activity: Notice how you like to impress others and also emulate successful people; reveal more of your true self and follow what you really want, not what you think you should want because it confers social status.

Development activity: Give yourself two hours each week to do only what you truly want to do, not what you have to do or think you should do. Only do what is your heart's desire and experience what happens. At first, identifying what you really want may be challenging, but keep doing this activity weekly until something emerges. Don't stop when you do discover what you really want; keep doing this activity until you no longer want to do it. What you desire or want will change over time.

PART 5 REACHING RECONCILIATION

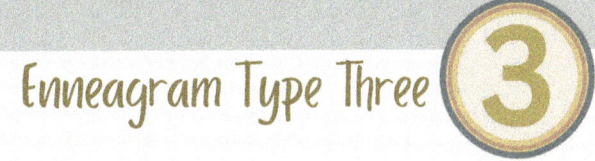

Enneagram Type Three

One-to-One Three subtypes ("masculinity/femininity") try to draw important individuals to them by appearing highly attractive and successful and also make great efforts to help these others achieve success, as if these accomplishments reflect positively on their own importance.

One-to-One Three subtype trigger: Feeling rejected by someone you have your sights set on as a partner (romantic, friendship, business, or other).

Awareness activity: Notice how you live for and through your partners by appealing to and supporting them; learn to support yourself better.

Development activity: When you observe yourself trying to make yourself attractive and appealing to someone important you either have or want to have a close relationship with, stop and ask yourself: *Why am I trying so hard to make myself so attractive to this person? Is this really me? Do I truly want relationships where I can't show or be the real me?*

As a Three, what do I think is my primary subtype?

Am I willing to engage in the recommended activity for my subtype?

What would help and hinder me in doing this?

PART 5 REACHING RECONCILIATION

SUBTYPE-BASED DEVELOPMENT

Enneagram Type Four

Emotional passion of ENVY Consciously and unconsciously comparing yourself to others to determine how you measure up and why you don't feel good enough, then feeling deficient, superior, or both, as well as suffering from these comparisons

Self-Preservation Four subtypes ("reckless/dauntless") bear their suffering in silence to prove that they are good enough by virtue of enduring pain and also engage in nonstop activity or even reckless behavior as a way to feel excited, energized, and not feel melancholic.

Self-Preservation Four subtype trigger: Feeling forced to stand still and deal with your deeper feelings rather than engaging in a stir of activities that help you escape.

Awareness activity: Notice how you feel you have to go through life and suffer on your own; embrace more fun and let more people in.

Development activity: Make an assessment of activities in which you engage for the excitement or risk-related effects versus the activities you do for pure enjoyment. Stop the ones that adrenalize you or involve risk and do the ones — or add new ones — that are satisfying and rewarding.

Social Four subtypes ("shame") focus on their deficiencies and on earning understanding and appreciation for their suffering, particularly from the groups to which they belong.

Social Four subtype trigger: Feeling shamed, embarrassed, or ostracized from a group you want to be part of.

Awareness activity: Notice how and when you feel inadequate and inferior; relax your negative self-judgments.

Development activity: When you experience yourself sitting in a pool of pondering your feelings, no matter what they are, take some action instead. Any action will do, but affirming action related to what you are pondering is even better.

PART 5 REACHING RECONCILIATION

Enneagram Type Four

One-to-One Four subtypes ("competition") express their needs and feelings outwardly and are highly competitive in order to gain attention, to be heard, to be acknowledged, and to feel understood.

One-to-One Four subtype trigger: Competing and losing at just about anything – for example, a debate, a competition, a romantic desire.

Awareness activity: Notice your competitiveness and the "transporting" of your suffering to others; pursue what's underneath your feelings, particularly when you feel competitive.

Development activity: Notice how your competitive feelings arise when someone else is getting attention. Pay attention to what you do next, whether you, for example, completely withdraw or do the opposite and say or do something that brings the attention back to you. Explore what you are really feeling underneath your behavior.

As a Four, what do I think is my primary subtype?

Am I willing to engage in the recommended activity for my subtype?

What would help and hinder me in doing this?

PART 5 REACHING RECONCILIATION

SUBTYPE-BASED DEVELOPMENT

Enneagram Type Five

Emotional passion of AVARICE The intense drive to acquire information, knowledge and wisdom and to avoid intrusion and loss of energy, but also to guard and preserve the resources you think you might need

Self-Preservation Five subtypes ("castle") are highly concerned with being intruded upon and being overextended physically and energetically. For this reason, they minimize their direct involvement with others at the same time as they hoard their scarce resources.

Self-Preservation Five subtype trigger: Feeling forced to engage when you want to withdraw.

Awareness activity: Notice how you retract, hide and create strong and non-penetrable boundaries, thus limiting your contact with others; engage more in the outside world.

Development activity: Is there a place where you go for solitude without any intrusion from anyone or anything else, likely in your living space? This is what is meant by the word "castle," a protected space where you control how long you stay and also control who has access to you. Once you've identified this space, track when you go there, how long you spend there, and what you actually do when you are there. After a week of tracking your time in this protected space, gradually spend a little less time there and more time where there are others around you.

Social Five subtypes ("totem") find, develop and guard or hoard their strong connections with people and groups who share their super-ideals and values, but become disengaged from these groups if they discover they are not fully aligned with these higher-order beliefs.

Social Five subtype trigger: Being excluded or marginalized from a social group with which you identify due to shared values and beliefs.

Awareness activity: Notice how your quest for connection through knowledge and ideas allows you to connect with some people, particularly in groups, but also limits your contact with many others; engage with more people in a variety of ways.

Development activity: Develop new interests, especially ones that you can do with others, that are not particularly linked to higher ideals and shared beliefs. This will help you expand your interests and unlink your interests to only those based on lofty ideals. Learn to enjoy doing things soley for the sake of doing them.

PART 5 REACHING RECONCILIATION

Enneagram Type Five

One-to-One Five subtypes ("confidence") search for a strong, deep connection with one other person whom they trust and can share confidences or private information, then want to keep the other person and this special relationship for themselves only.

One-to-One Five subtype trigger: Feeling bereft when a special partner disappoints you deeply – for example, wants to leave the relationship or violates your confidence in some way.

Awareness activity: Notice how your high expectations and testing of others limit your relationships; take the risk of sharing your real feelings with more people.

Development activity: Make a list of your requirements for those you are interested in and willing to have a special relationship – in other words, those with whom you have enough confidence that you are willing to share your private or confidential thoughts and feelings. Ask yourself this: *Why do I have such a list? What is its purpose? What do I gain from having this list and how does adhering to it limit me and the possible relationships I could have?*

As a Five, what do I think is my primary subtype?

Am I willing to engage in the recommended activity for my subtype?

What would help and hinder me in doing this?

PART 5 REACHING RECONCILIATION

SUBTYPE-BASED DEVELOPMENT

Enneagram Type Six

The emotional passion of FEAR Fearing that something bad or negative will happen, and doubting that others are trustworthy or that you and they are capable of meeting the challenges that arise

Self-Preservation Six subtypes ("warmth") have an intense need to feel protected from danger, often utilizing the family, a surrogate family or support groups to provide this, and they use their friendliness to feel safe. They think no harm will come to them if they are warm toward others and also believe there is safety being part of a group.

Self-Preservation Six subtype trigger: Not having your worries affirmed by others, and especially having your worries invalidated by others.

Awareness activity: Notice how often you question everything and act overly warm toward others as a way to feel safe; learn to relax your self-doubt and the need to ingratiate yourself.

Development activity: Ponder how you use your self-doubt to feel safe, making sure you've considered multiple pathways so you can choose the route with the least probable negative outcomes. The paradox is that your continuous doubt actually makes you feel less certain and safe. This paradox becomes an endless loop.

Social Six subtypes ("duty") focus on rules, regulations, and prescribed ways of behaving within their social environment in order to keep their behavior acceptable and to not get chastised or punished by authority figures.

Social Six subtype trigger: Anticipating getting in trouble with an authority figure.

Awareness activity: Notice how you rely on rules and overly accommodating relationships with authorities to feel safe; learn to relax your reliance on rules, your compliant relationships with authority figures, and your overly strong sense of duty to groups to which you belong.

Development activity: Contemplate the word "dutiful" and how you have gone about doing your duty throughout and in various aspects of your life. While responsibility is a good quality, always doing your duty for others can be limiting for you in terms of the choices you make for yourself. Doing your duty for the group may lead you take action on behalf of the group that you think serves the group, but may unintentionally harm you and even the group. For example, you may overwork or over-volunteer and exhaust yourself. You may speak up on behalf of the group and get yourself in trouble with those in charge, even to the point of getting fired.

PART 5 REACHING RECONCILIATION

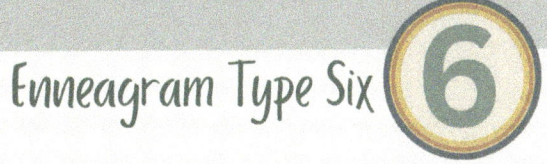

Enneagram Type Six

One-to-One Six subtypes ("strength/beauty") deny own anxieties by pushing against their fear, appearing bold, confident, charismatic, and sometimes fierce or fearless. This subtype of Six is often referred to as a counter-fear or counter-phobic Six because they try to prove, often unconsciously, that they have no fear.

One-to-One Six subtype trigger: Feeling extremely fearful to such a degree that their counter-fear response is not enough to dispel it.

Awareness activity: Notice how you rely on "shows of strength" and being compelling and charismatic as a way for you to feel safe; learn to let go of your armor in whatever form it appears.

Development activity: The term "strength" and the term "beauty" have an importance for you to think about in terms of how you go against your fear to show you are not afraid. "Strength" can take the form of extreme physical activities, aggressively confronting authority figures, intense body building, and more. "Beauty" can manifest in extreme attention to attractiveness, high levels of charisma, and more. Pay attention to your particular forms of "strength/beauty" and delve deeply into the fears and anxieties that lie underneath.

As a Six, what do I think is my primary subtype?

Am I willing to engage in the recommended activity for my subtype?

What would help and hinder me in doing this?

PART 5 REACHING RECONCILIATION

SUBTYPE-BASED DEVELOPMENT

Enneagram Type Seven

The emotional passion of GLUTTONY The insatiable thirst for new and constant stimulation through exciting ideas, people and experiences, thus enabling the avoidance of feeling painful emotions, facing difficult situations, and denying any sense of being limited or constrained

Self-Preservation Seven subtypes ("keepers of the castle") create close networks of family, friends, and colleagues to keep themselves feeling stimulated and secure, as well as to generate new and intriguing opportunities to pursue.

Self-Preservation Seven subtype trigger: Feeling thwarted in satisfying specific desires, especially physical desires.

Awareness activity: Notice how new opportunities and physical pleasure or satisfaction are so important to you; explore your anxiety and pain that lie underneath.

Development activity: Assess the kinds of physical stimulation you crave the most. What are they? How often do they occur? What factors, internal or external, activate them? Next, every time you are about to pursue the particular kinds of physical stimulation you crave, pause and ask yourself what you are really feeling.

Social Seven subtypes ("sacrifice") sacrifice their own needs for satisfaction and stimulation, at least temporarily, in service of the group or an important ideal by postponing their gratification, but they also want explicit recognition for their sacrifice and to get their needs met shortly after their sacrifice.

Social Seven subtype trigger: Not receiving explicit thanks for the sacrifices that you make on behalf of groups.

Awareness activity: Notice how you want to be acknowledged for your sacrifice and goodness; explore the feelings below your explanations and rationales for your sacrifice.

Development Activity: When you delay your desires or needs on behalf of a group, what are the explanations or stories you tell yourself about this? These may be partially accurate, but beneath them may be other motivations that are useful for you to explore. For example, does your sacrifice make you feel like a good person rather than someone more focused on themselves and their desires? Does your sacrifice give you a special role in the group that you would otherwise not have?

PART 5 REACHING RECONCILIATION

Enneagram Type Seven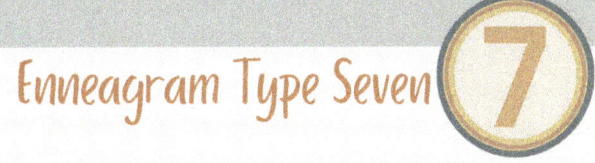

One-to-One Seven subtypes ("suggestibility/fascination") need to see the stark reality of the world in the most positive ways, as if they are using rose-colored glasses to embellish reality so they can live in a super-optimistic, dream-like state, and this is particularly true when it comes to relationships.

One-to-One Seven subtype trigger: Deep disappointment in romantic or intimate encounters that don't live up to your romanticized ideas.

Awareness activity: Notice how you live in an idealized and embellished version of reality; ground yourself in unfiltered reality.

Development activity: Think about the most important relationships you've had in your life, especially those you consider romantic ones. Have you created an idealized, romanticized sense of a wonderful relationship in your mind, only to find that real life does not measure up? If so, consider how your idealized or overly positive view of relationships may hinder your ability to experience fully satisfying relationships with people in your life now.

As a Seven, what do I think is my primary subtype?

Am I willing to engage in the recommended activity for my subtype?

What would help and hinder me in doing this?

PART 5 REACHING RECONCILIATION

SUBTYPE-BASED DEVELOPMENT

Enneagram Type Eight 8

The emotional passion of LUST Denying anxiety and sadness by engaging in a variety of self-satisfying behaviors and doing so in an excessive way

Self-Preservation Eights subtypes ("survival") get what they think they need for survival, become highly frustrated, intolerant, and angry when the fulfillment of their needs are thwarted, are attuned to power and influence dynamics, and tend be quieter than the other two subtypes of Eight.

Self-Preservation Eight subtype trigger: Feeling a loss of personal and positional influence and power.

Awareness activity: Notice your need to be strong, self-reliant and strategic; learn to strategize less and verbalize your needs and rely on others more.

Development activity: Pay attention to how often you observe and are attuned to the power and influence dynamics that occur in a variety of contexts. Ask yourself why you do this on such a consistent basis, how this serves you, and how it might get in the way of your full engagement with other people. Why the need to observe and strategize? Does it make you feel more in control and less vulnerable? Explore this last question in depth.

Social Eight subtypes ("solidarity") vigorously protect others from unjust and unfair authorities and systems and challenge social norms, while also seeking power, influence, and pleasure.

Social Eight subtype trigger: Social justice being thwarted, particularly toward or within communities with which you identify.

Awareness activity: Notice your need to be strong and to protect other people; allow yourself to need and be supported by others.

Development activity: Consider how often you step into leadership roles and volunteer to engage in projects or activities that come from your sense of responsibility to groups. Do you even like groups or are you ambivalent about them? When you are about to step up and into roles and responsibilities that you don't like or want or are ambivalent about, ask yourself why you are doing this. When you are energized and invigorated by influential roles in groups and are about to say yes to a role, ask yourself why you get so charged up about this. Pay attention to how functioning in this way may not really satisfy you in the long run and may exhaust you.

PART 5 REACHING RECONCILIATION

Enneagram Type Eight

One-to-One Eight subtypes ("possession") are rebellious, provocative, emotional, intense, and passionate, draw others to them and derive their power and influence from being at the center of events and the lives of others.

One-to-One Eight subtype trigger: Feeling vulnerable when a loved one moves on or leaves you in any way.

Awareness activity: Notice your need to provoke, to be potent, to possess the ones you love and to be at the center of and control everything if you can; manage your intensity and be both more present and pure.

Development activity: Do you want all of something or someone you love or care about? This is what the word "possession" means. Although you may not think of your desires as possessive, those on the receiving end often do. To have more balanced and spacious relationships, relax your needs and actions when you start to want to have all of something or someone. Breathe and tell yourself this: *Let me give my desires and the other person more freedom and space.*

As a Eight, what do I think is my primary subtype?

Am I willing to engage in the recommended activity for my subtype?

What would help and hinder me in doing this?

PART 5 REACHING RECONCILIATION

SUBTYPE-BASED DEVELOPMENT

Enneagram Type Nine — 9

The emotional passion of LAZINESS Avoiding conflict by numbing yourself and not paying attention to your own inner responses, thus disabling you from knowing what you think, feel, want and the right action to take

Self-Preservation Nine subtypes ("appetite") use the comfort of routine, rhythmic, and pleasant activities to not pay attention to themselves.

Self-Preservation Nine subtype trigger: Having your routines and comfort interrupted.

Awareness activity: Notice the subtle clues, particularly the physical and somatic ones, to your deep anger, energy and vitality; relax your need for comfort and move toward action.

Development activity: Identify the physical behaviors that you engage in regularly that you find comforting, such as rocking back and forth physically, nodding your head on a regular basis, eating for comfort, and sleeping when you are distressed. Once you know what these are, every time you are just about to do one of them, ask yourself instead what you are feeling and spend time exploring your emotions.

Social Nine subtypes ("participation") work extremely hard on behalf of a group, organization, or cause as a way to belong and as a way of not focusing on themselves.

Social Nine subtype trigger: Being marginalized from a group in which you have invested abundant time and energy.

Awareness activity: Notice how you dive into work or activities as a way of belonging to groups; slow down and honor your feelings, needs, and desires.

Development activity: You may have already recognized that you work really hard on behalf of groups, but often don't recognize the level of your stress until you are exhausted. Pay much more attention to the early warning signs of stress and stop engaging in those activities to give yourself time to reflect on these questions: *What makes it so hard for me to not throw myself into these activities? What would happen if I were more deliberate in what I chose to do?*

PART 5 REACHING RECONCILIATION

 Enneagram Type Nine

One-to-One Nine subtypes ("fusion/union") join, merge or fuse with important individuals as a way of not paying attention to their own thoughts, feelings, needs, and deep desires.

One-to-One Nine subtype trigger: Being left by someone with whom you have fully merged.

Awareness activity: Notice how you vacate yourself - lose your sense of self - by merging with special others; focus on who you are and express yourself.

Development activity: Think of what happens with you when these fused relationships come to an end. What are you left with? Because many relationships either end or change in some way, do you want to be left with deep heartache, confusion, and a very large loss of sense of self? If you don't, keeping a solid sense of a separate self is essential. Keep asking yourself these questions: *Who am I? What do I think? What do I feel? What do I want? What do I like? What do I dislike?*

As a Nine, what do I think is my primary subtype?

Am I willing to engage in the recommended activity for my subtype?

What would help and hinder me in doing this?

PART 5 REACHING RECONCILIATION
CATALYTIC CONVERSIONS THROUGH SUBTYPES

If you want to use subtypes for tranformation and not just for comfort or progress, you can use this process. A car engine's catalytic converter is part of the exhaust system that transforms toxic pollutants into non-toxic substances like water vapor and carbon dioxide. Similarly, we can convert the energy of our subtype reactivity into another state.

This activity requires that you be in your subtype-based reactive state. That way, you can do the activity in real time to experience it fully. You can also do this activity if you remember a time when you felt highly activated in your subtype-based reactivity.

CATALYTIC CONVERSION PROCESS

Stay in the experience of being highly activated in your subtype behavior, but don't act on your behavior or change your reactive impulse.

Stop and pause, breathe deeply, and hold the impulse or vibrancy of your response within your body, neither acting on it nor trying to make it go away. Simply hold the impulse to act and allow the vibrancy and energy of it to fill your body.

Keep breathing while you do this and notice what happens. The impulse will often slowly leave, almost like evaporation, or even change into something really positive. This is sometimes referred to as a catalytic conversion, and it is very powerful.

Do this activity every time your subtype impulse emerges. The more you do this in real time, the bigger and deeper the impact.

Reflect on this experience.

PART 5 REACHING RECONCILIATION

MANDALAS

A mandala, an art form found in many cultures and traditions, represents wholeness, unity, and the deeper facets of life. The word mandala comes from the ancient Indian Sanskrit language, meaning circle or sacred circle. They usually involve circular patterns with repeating shapes, radiating from a central point outward. In Jungian psychology, mandalas represent the psyche's search for wholeness and integration.

These examples are to inspire you as you create your own mandalas.

PART 5 REACHING RECONCILIATION

CREATE YOUR MANDALA

This is an invitation to create a mandala that reflects where you've been on your journey, where you are now, and where you are going.

Start with self-reflection

What colors do you love?

What shapes speak to you?

What words make your heart sing, make your body feel complete or make your mind tingle?

Are there objects or images or metaphors that you love and have special meaning for you?

What is fundamental to your development journey at this point in your life?

Are there particular paradoxes and intriguing complexities in your life right now?

If you had a phrase that captured your development right now, what would it be?

PART 5 REACHING RECONCILIATION

CREATE YOUR MANDALA

You can use the circle as your canvas to express your development journey, unless you prefer another shape.

The center might represent your essence, Enneagram type, or an evocative symbol.

Concentric rings, symbols, or pathways might show movement, tension, growth or time.

Use metaphors if you like – a tree, mountain, river, phoenix, labyrinth, etc.

Include words, colors, shapes, and textures or anything you choose.

Mandalas are personal and non-linear, so don't concern yourself with it being correct in any way. It is simply yours. It's a visual, intuitive process.

PART 5 REACHING RECONCILIATION

DEVELOPMENT PLANNING PROCESS

We hope this 5-step development plan inspires you on your journey.

Step 1
Self-Assessment

1) Put an X on the map that best reflects where you are on the journey to your true self.

Write your self-reflections here.

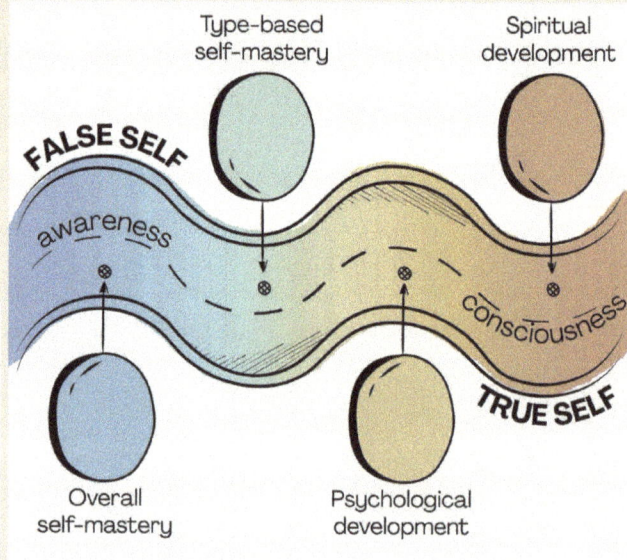

2) Place a O (circle) on the map that best reflects where you aspire to be in the future. Before you place your O on the map, select your desired timeframe.

☐ 3 months   ☐ 6 months   ☐ 1 year   ☐ Other _____

3) If you let yourself dream, how do you imagine you'll be in that future time? Put your thoughts here.

PART 5 REACHING RECONCILIATION

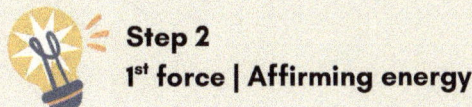

Step 2
1st force | Affirming energy

What am I moving toward? What inside me wants this change and growth?

Step 3
2nd force | Denying energy

What challenges or constrains me? What inner or outer resistance am I facing?

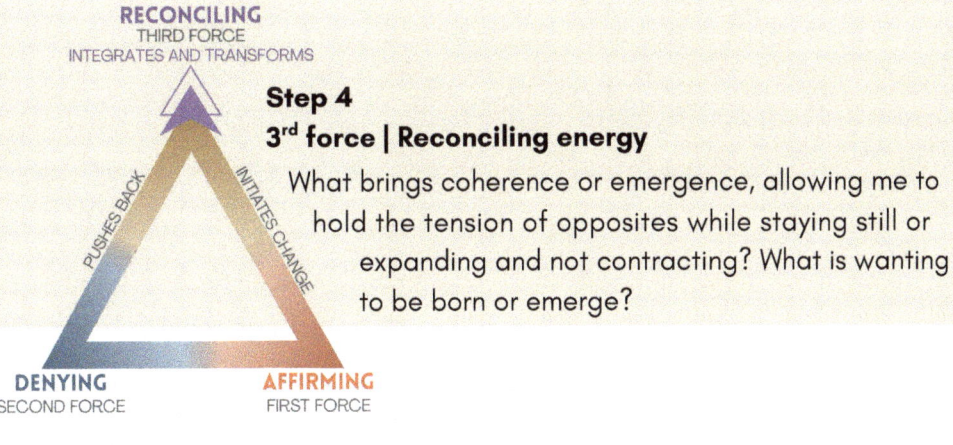

Step 4
3rd force | Reconciling energy

What brings coherence or emergence, allowing me to hold the tension of opposites while staying still or expanding and not contracting? What is wanting to be born or emerge?

PART 5 REACHING RECONCILIATION

Step 5
Development by Design Practice Plan

"Tell me, what is it you plan to do with your one wild and precious life?" – Mary Oliver

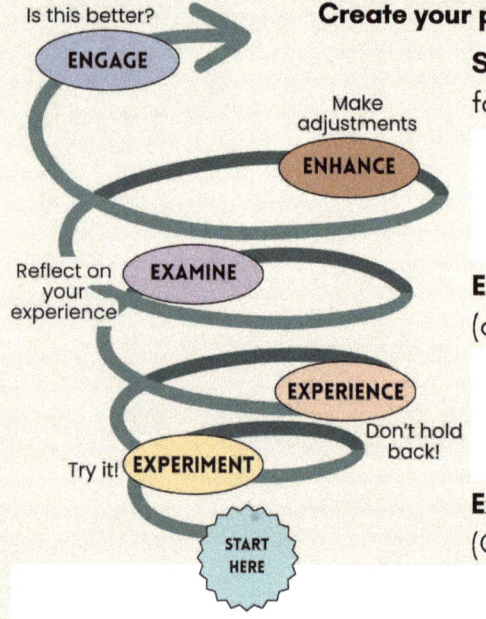

Create your plan!

Start here: Based on the three energetic forces, what is my growth area?

Experiment: What am I actually going to do (activities, exercises, etc.)

Experience: Here is my experience doing it. (Complete this after you have tried it.)

Examine: These are my reflections on this experience.

Enhance: What adjustment do I want to make? If none, answer the last question. If some adjustments, experiment with these changes, then move to the last question.

Engage: How did this work?

Start date   **Completion date**

Note: The Enneagram Development Guide (by Ginger Lapid-Bogda, PhD) is full of 50+ development activities specifically targeted for each type and organized by areas for development.

PART 5 REACHING RECONCILIATION

PART 5 HIGHLIGHTS

REMEMBER
Integration and wholeness require both the affirming and denying forces

Reconciliation requires being awake and surrendering

The experience of reconciliation, integration and wholeness is an aspiration, a journey, and a process

DO'S
Productively access all three Centers of Intelligence

Embrace paradox

Allow emergent wisdom

DONT'S
Push

Judge

Avoid

REFLECTIONS
"The real voyage of discovery consists not in seeking new landscapes, but in having new eyes."
- Marcel Proust

"Don't push the river. It flows by itself."
- Fritz Perls

BEYOND THE BOOK

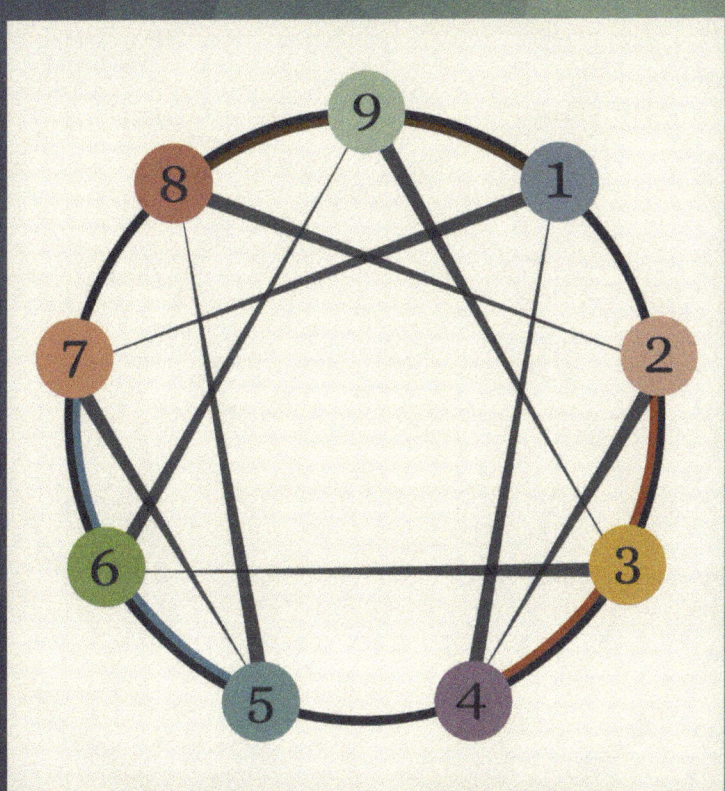

PART SIX

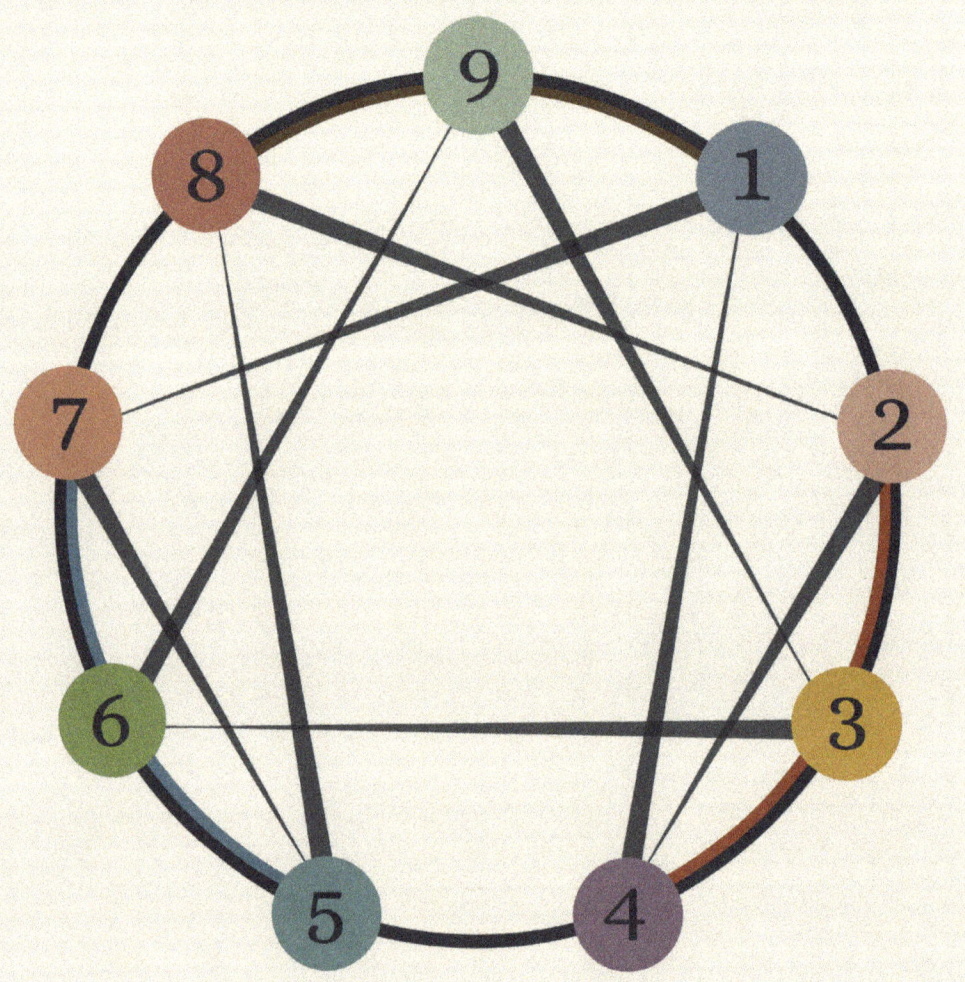

THE BOOK CREATORS

THE AUTHOR

Ginger Lapid-Bogda, PhD, is an internationally respected Enneagram teacher, author, coach, and consultant whose work has shaped how people understand development and transformation. Blending psychology, spirituality, and practical application, she helps individuals, teams and organizations grow from the inside out - with wisdom, humor, and heart. The author of ten influential Enneagram books, Ginger is known for translating profound insights from the Enneagram into clear, actionable practices that actually change lives. Her newest book, *Development by Design*, distills her decades of experience into a framework for authentic, sustainable growth. Known for her warmth and insight, she is a longtime thought leader in the global Enneagram community and continues to teach, write, and inspire others to do the deep work that leads to true transformation.

THE ILLUSTRATOR

Gwen Baker-Yuill is Creative Director and Program Operations lead for The Enneagram in Business. Trained as a commercial sculptor, she has created three-dimensional work for Disney, Mattel, and Warner Bros. and has taught middle and high school art, theater, and English. Gwen illustrates and designs educational materials, builds and manages websites, and loves exploring new digital platforms. She supports the production of books, programs, and online learning resources.

THE ENNEAGRAM IN BUSINESS

Founded in 2004 by Ginger Lapid-Bogda, PhD, The Enneagram in Business is a premier provider of Enneagram resources for use in organizations across the globe. Their books, professional services, training resources, and digital tools are well-known for their accuracy, practicality, and creativity. They also have a global network of top-quality Enneagram professionals (EIBN) providing services worldwide.
TheEnneagramInBusiness.com • info@TheEnneagramInBusiness.com

BEYOND THE BOOK RESOURCES

TRAINING PROGRAMS

Development by Design
Experience our programs inspired by this book designed for deeper learning.

Development by Design: Introduction
An introduction to Development by Design, familiarizing you with the three forces of transformation – affirming, denying and reconciling
TheEnneagramInBusiness.com

Development by Design: Intensive
In-depth, immersive and transformative sessions taking you through the transformation journey using the Enneagram and Gurdjieff's Law of Three
TheEnneagramInBusiness.com

Development by Design: Advanced
A deepening of the transformative experience of Development by Design, only for past participants of Development by Design: Intensive
TheEnneagramInBusiness.com

PROFESSIONAL CERTIFICATION PROGRAMS

Since 2004, we've certified thousands of Enneagram professionals worldwide: programs in coaching (ICF-accredited), leadership, teams, subtypes, and more. IEA-accredited School with Distinction.
TheEnneagramInBusiness.com/store

ELECTRONIC LEARNING PLATFORMS

Enneagram Experiences (EE)
Learn Enneagram theory through interactive, gamified content – accurate, engaging, and fun: seven topics.
EnneagramExperiences.com

Enneagram Learning Portal (ELP)
A subscription-based platform covering Enneagram foundations, professional development, and applications.
EnneagramLearningPortal.com

ENNEAGRAM TRAINING TOOLS

Full-color training materials to make teaching easier and learning memorable.
30 hard copy tools
8 virtual tools
TheEnneagramInBusiness.com/store

ENNEAGRAM FABRIC MAPS

Recreate the experience from this book – washable, portable, and available in five different designs and two sizes.
TheEnneagramInBusiness.com/store

BEYOND THE BOOK RESOURCES

OTHER BOOKS BY GINGER LAPID-BOGDA PHD

The Enneagram Development Guide, 3rd Edition

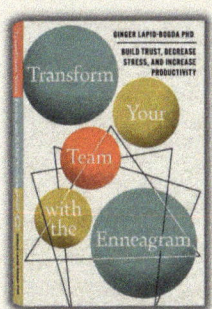
Transform Your Team with the Enneagram

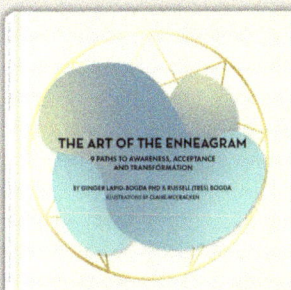
The Art of the Enneagram with Russell (Tres) Bogda

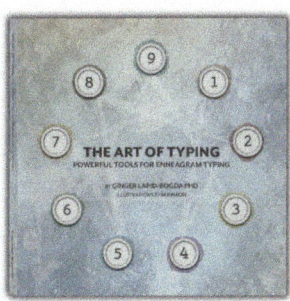
The Art of Typing

The Enneagram Coloring Book

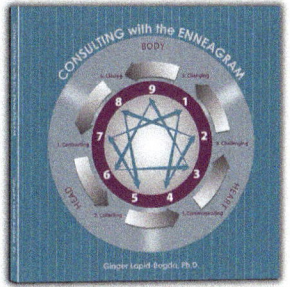
Consulting with the Enneagram

Bringing Out the Best in Everyone You Coach

What Type of Leader Are You?

Bringing Out the Best in Yourself at Work

NOTES

www.ingramcontent.com/pod-product-compliance
Ingram Content Group UK Ltd.
Pitfield, Milton Keynes, MK11 3LW, UK
UKHW060214240426
12048UKWH00031BB/1715